What You Can Do With a Word

300 Classroom Reading Activities

Dorothy Raymond

Academic Therapy Publications
Novato, California

Academic Therapy Publications
20 Commercial Boulevard
Novato, California 94947

Books, tests, and materials for and about the
learning disabled
International Standard Book Number: 0-87879-269-4

0 9 8 7 6 5 4 3 2
0 9 8 7 6 5 4 3 2

INTRODUCTION

One of the most difficult jobs faced by classroom teachers is to provide suitable learning activities for students with reading problems, particularly those with learning disabilities. They are our most misunderstood students. They seem to be so capable, yet they do not learn even with the typical remedial reading techniques. This means that the usual resources available to classroom teachers will be inadequate, and many classroom teachers will feel helpless and frustrated.

Students with severe reading disabilities do not profit from the usual workbooks and work sheets for a number of reasons. To begin with, the format of most presents a cluttered appearance which in itself is overwhelming. Then the directions are often too complicated for the learning disabled. The something to be written "on the line below," for example, may show up on most any line "below" including the decorative border at the bottom of the page. To further complicate the problem, most work sheets have more than one activity and thus, more than one set of directions. The most serious disadvantage of these materials, though, is the vocabulary load. Students with reading disabilities, particularly in the beginning stages of tutoring, know very few words and then only the words that they have been specifically taught. Even supposing that the words taught were in the workbook, they would be presented much too quickly.

Teachers need suggestions that can be used with any and all students. They need worthwhile activities to reinforce reading instruction that require little or no teacher preparation, and are adaptable to all learners. The activities in this book have been chosen to meet that need.

ACKNOWLEDGMENTS

The activities suggested in this book have been collected over a period of twenty years in a public school system where "mainstreaming" was the policy before we had a word to describe it. The learning disabled were and are tutored individually outside the classroom, but spend most of their time in the classroom. Teachers would ask for suggestions and the tutors and I would make them. Many of mine were adapted from activities first observed in primary classrooms so my first acknowledgment goes to the hundreds of classroom teachers in the Waterville, Maine Public School System who willingly or unknowingly shared their ideas with me.

Grateful acknowledgment also goes to the teachers who accepted the suggestions and to their students who had reading disabilities.

Over the years, the learning disability tutors have made special efforts to help teachers provide specific assignments for the students they tutored. Their efforts are also acknowledged and particular thanks go to Marie Christensen, Mary Clark, Geneva Padham, Chris Rasmussen, Anne Rosenthal, Sherril Saulter, and Jean Spencer. Special thanks go to Winnie Kierstead who made many practical suggestions first as a learning disability tutor and then as a reading specialist in the Title I program.

Listing and classifying these suggestions was made possible by an ESEA Title IV-C Mini-Grant from the Maine

Department of Educational and Cultural Services. However, the content and opinions expressed do not necessarily reflect the position or policy of the Department. Working with me on the grant, Elaine Bean, a reading specialist in the Title I program, contributed many ideas. The clerical work was done by Nancy Decker and Lorraine Smith.

TABLE OF CONTENTS

DEDICATION

To the memory of

Frankie Merrick

June 28, 1968 - June 13, 1979

PART I
SIGHT VOCABULARY

SIGHT VOCABULARY

Students with learning disabilities need many experiences with words in order to remember them. Many students, particularly at first, will feel more comfortable doing the same type of activity over and over. This is especially true of those who have difficulty following directions. The fifty activities for SIGHT VOCABULARY may be used in any order, but the listing is approximately in ascending order of difficulty.

Remember that these are follow-up activities that can be used in a classroom. Students will have to be taught the words first. Learning disability specialists have their own favorite ways of doing this. We have found the most successful and reliable method to be the Fernald technique, particularly the first three "stages." Those planning to use this technique should prepare themselves by studying Grace Fernald's book, *Remedial Techniques in Basic School Subjects* (McGraw-Hill Book Co., 1943; Reissued 1971).

There are four "stages" for learning words. In the first one, the student, using one or two fingers, traces over the word while saying it. The word is not repeated over and over, but each part is pronounced once as tracing is begun on that part. The student traces as many times as necessary to be able to write it correctly without looking at the copy. Then the word is written. The student is never allowed to see a word incorrectly written so if a mistake is made, the tutor immediately stops the student and the word learning process begins again. We teach all words in cursive writing regardless of the age of the student. After a word has been written correctly twice in succession, it is printed on a card and placed in a "word box." The next day, the student sees the word first in typewritten form. After a while a student will want to try learning a word without tracing it. This is Fernald's second "stage." The tutor still writes the word as in the first "stage." The student looks at it, pronouncing it by syllables, and then writes it.

In the third "stage," the tutor does not have to write the word. The student is able to write it after studying the printed form. From the very beginning, with the first word a student wants to learn, we look all words up in a dictionary, and show them to the student. Thus, going from "stage" two to three is as natural as going from "stage" one to two.

Fernald's fourth "stage" is the ability to recognize new words by noting their similarity to words already learned. Long before our students reach this "stage" we teach them phonics, using their own word cards. The lessons vary, depending on the needs and capabilities of the students. If a student has a number of words beginning with b and chooses to learn butterfly, for example, the tutor would ask the student to listen to the first sound and tell what letter to turn to in a dictionary to locate that word.

Another reason for our success, perhaps really the main reason, is the creative approach used in the tutoring sessions. From the first question, "What word would you like to learn?" students write their own stories. This means that the interest level and language used are as mature as the learner. It is a language experience approach modified only in that the student first dictates a story to a tutor and then writes it, learning every word.

No matter how words are first learned, it is necessary to practice reading them in many different ways. That is the purpose of these fifty suggestions.

Students will need a place to keep their words. Plastic crayon boxes are ideal for this purpose as they are just the right size, colorful, and seem to last forever. You will need oaktag strips about one inch wide and three inches long for the word cards. Color is not necessary, but it does add interest. We use a different color for each report card period to make it easy to note progress throughout the year. If your school has a print shop in the high school or vocational school, you not only can get all the cards you want, but you will also find that they will cut the cards for you. You will also need some felt tip markers for writing the words, and a supply of pictures. The pictures can be taken from old spelling, language, and reading workbooks which you can get from primary teachers. These, as well as pictures from magazines, need only be torn out as the students can cut out the ones they want to use.

1. Have the students choose the words they want to learn. The first word a student chooses usually indicates a personal interest. Use that interest as a focus for more words by starting a mobile. (Example: If the first word were hockey, suggest that the student think of another word to learn related to hockey. Then make a mobile of pictures and words.)

2. Provide students with pictures that would correspond with the words in their word boxes. Have them match the words to the pictures.

   This is the easiest to do for nouns. For other words, provide pictures, but let the student choose the most appropriate ones and tell why they are appropriate. *Around* might be a "fence *around* a field;" *in* might be "a man sitting *in* a car;" *pretty* might be a "pretty flower." The purpose of this exercise is not only to give practice in recognizing words but also to provide opportunities for the student to think about different meanings for the words. This aids recall.

3. Make a duplicate set of a student's word cards. Student places both sets of cards on a desk and matches them.
   At first, the words should all be printed in manuscript on both sets. After the student can match manuscript to manuscript, then have one set in manuscript and one set typed.

4. Here is another way to get students to look carefully at their words. Type the words in a column. Then type another column next to the first one, but have the words in a different order. The student connects similar words with a colored crayon. Example:

car	mountain
hike	car
lake	lake
mountain	hike

5. Have an egg box ready for this activity. When the student knows twelve words print each word on a card. Cut the words apart by letters and place the letters in an egg box, one word in each section. For example, if one word were "come" you would cut it so that the four letters were separated, and you would put those letters in one section of the egg box. The student removes the letters and makes the word. (The student probably will need to refer to the original word cards to do this.) Note that using different colored inks and paper for each word will avoid confusion.

6. Print the student's name, putting each letter on a separate card. Place the name along the top of a desk. Have the student find words in word box that begin with each of the letters. Ask, "Which letter had the most words?"

7. Have students arrange all their words by first letters. Which letter had the most words? Have members of the class compare.

8. Have students bring in words they can read from cans and food boxes. Paste the words on a poster: WORDS WE CAN READ.

9. Make up five descriptive sentences using words the student knows. Put the sentences on strips of paper. Have the student draw pictures to illustrate the sentences and then write the sentences under the appropriate pictures. Examples: See the red car. My hat is red. It was a little yellow kitten.

10. Have students try to draw pictures to illustrate their words. Give them little squares of paper. They could put a word along the bottom edge and then draw a picture or they could have a word on one side of the paper and the illustration on the other.

11. Tell students to look at the words in their boxes. Find the longest word, the shortest word, the word with the most syllables. This requires them to look carefully at their words. The students could write the words on the chalkboard. To locate the longest word, for example, one word is put on the board. If another student has a longer word, that word is put on the board and the first word is erased.

12. Give students alphabet noodles and have them paste the noodles on paper to spell words or sentences. At this stage, they will probably be reconstructing words they have in their boxes. This type of activity forces them to examine their words carefully.

13. Have the student shape letters out of clay to make a new word. (Be sure that the student knows what the word is.)

14. Choose a noun from a student's box. Provide the student with letter cards that include the letters in the

word and some extra letters. The student is to match the letters to the word, paste them along the bottom of a piece of drawing paper and then draw a picture to illustrate the word.

Example: If the noun were *butterfly,* the student would be given the following letters on separate cards — b, u, t, t, e, r, f, l, y plus any other additional letters such as d, n, g, c, h. Copying the word from the original card, the student would arrange the letters correctly to spell *butterfly,* paste them on drawing paper, and draw a picture of a butterfly.

15. Tell students to look at all their words. Find two that rhyme, two that begin with the same letter, two that end the same. Other categories could be used such as colors, food, animals, feelings, etc.

16. Using a student's words, make a list with first or last or other letters missing. Have the students locate the word in the box and then write in the missing letters.

    Examples: sch_____ (school)
    boo__ (book)

17. Have students look in their word boxes for two-letter words. Have them make the words with letter cards, and copy them on a piece of paper. (Use the same directions for three-letter words, etc.)

18. Tell student to choose any word from word box. Find all the other words in the box that begin with the same letter. Now find all the words that begin with the next letter of the alphabet.

19. Have the student put all words in word box in alphabetical order. Is there a word for each letter?

What letters don't have words? Think of some words for those letters.

20. Have students keep an illustrated word book. Provide them with booklets in which the pages are labeled alphabetically. Students are to write each new word on the appropriate page and draw an illustration for the word. The words on the pages, of course, would not be in alphabetical order.

21. Students take words such as car, table, ball, mitten, from their word boxes that would be easy to illustrate and form plurals by adding *s*.

22. Give all students envelopes containing all the letters in their first and last names. Each letter is on a separate card. After they make their names, have them see how many other words they can make. As each word is made it should be written on a piece of paper. Who can make the most words? Settle all disputes by referring to a dictionary.

PAUL BRADFORD

lap of for rod pad brad lad lab fad fro drab board up fur purr ford add fad bad or burp load road roar pour oar rub odd rap bar far drop do

23. Write a descriptive sentence on a long card. Make a set of word cards that include the words in the sentence plus others that could be confused with the correct words.

A sentence might be, "The boy was playing ball with a big dog." Extra words in the set might be: try, saw, plays, doll, white, dig.

The student is to match the cards to the words in the sentence and paste them along the bottom of a piece of drawing paper. Then the student draws a picture to illustrate the sentence.

24. Choose five words from a student's word box and have the student add endings to make other words. Supply a list of possible endings like: s, ed, er, ers, est, ing.

    Examples: work works worked worker workers
    working
    plant plants planter planters planting
    find finds finding
    flower flowers flowering
    tall taller tallest

25. Have students put the numbers one to five on blank cards. Place the cards across the tops of their desks. Then have them arrange their word cards under the cards according to the number of syllables in the words.

1	2	3	4	5
puck	hockey	penalty	cooperate	international
skates		uniform	artificial	
			American	

26. Make sentence puzzles. Type sentences with a student's words. Cut apart and put in envelopes. (Use different colored paper for each sentence.) Have student arrange words to make sentences, and then write (copy) the sentences.

27. Choose five adjectives and five nouns from a student's box. Have the student put any two together that make sense and write (copy) on a piece of paper.

    1. Adjectives might be: pretty, red, wonderful, small, green.

    2. Nouns might be: bird, car, animal, boy, apple.

    3. Phrases might be: pretty bird, red car, wonderful animal.

28. Choose sets of words that are often confused by beginning readers. Make up sentences containing the

words but leave a blank space where the words belong. Make cards with the words on them. The student is to place the cards correctly and then read the sentences to someone. Examples of words: pretty, party; was, saw; come, came; where, there; went, want; on, no. Example of sentences for saw and was: We _____ a parade. Tom _____ going home. (Instead of reading the sentences, the student could write them.)

29. Take all words from word box that begin with a designated letter, all the *b* words, for example. Have student try to use as many as possible in one sentence.

    Example: The boy has a big blue boat.

30. Paste pictures of objects on one set of cards. Print the name of the objects on another set of cards. Put all of them in an envelope. Students match words to pictures.

31. Give the student five sentences leaving out one word in each sentence. Put the missing words on cards. Have the student place words correctly and then write (copy) the sentences.

32. Give students a list of words and phrases such as: a, two, many, one, a blue, four red, etc. They are to look through their boxes and add words that would make sense. (Examples: a car, two birds, many people.)

33. Many words can be recognized when different consonants are added to the beginning of phonograms or rhyming elements. For example, *at* can be made into cat, hat, bat, rat, mat, sat, fat, and pat. Use *word* phonograms that the students know and have them make new words by adding different initial consonants. Some word phonograms are: age, and, am, an, ate, all, as, at, eat, each, end, in, is, it, old, up.

34. Students look in newspapers or magazines for known words and underline them with a magic marker, crayon, or colored pencil. For example, give each student a news column or a full page grocery store advertisement.

35. Have a student choose a word from word box and write it on the chalkboard. Another student finds a word that begins with the last letter of the first word and writes it next to the first word, etc. (Example: rabbit, team, moth, hello, owl, lunch). Note that this can be an on-going activity as students find time or want to participate. The whole class does not have to sit and watch a few students add words.

36. Give students tape from calculating machines. Have them put a three-letter word at one end, and then add words by changing only one letter of the previous word. (Example: cat, ca*r*, *t*ar, *f*ar, fa*t* . . .)

37. Make games like concentration for students to play. Use words from their word boxes. To make a game of concentration to review sight words, choose eight or ten words and make two cards for each word. To play the game, the cards are shuffled and placed face down in rows. If there are ten words, there would be twenty cards, and they could be laid out in four rows of five cards each.

   X   X   X   X   X
   X   X   X   X   X
   X   X   X   X   X
   X   X   X   X   X

The first player turns over any two cards. If they match and the player can say the word, the player keeps them and turns over two more cards. If they don't match, or the player fails to recognize the word, the cards are placed face down again leaving them in the same place. The next player takes a chance. When all the cards are paired the game is over. The winner is the player with the most pairs.

38. Make charts, each with a separate heading. For example, We Can See, We Can Hear, We Can Smell, We Can Feel, We Can Taste. Students write words from their boxes under the proper headings. Some words will be in more than one column.

WE CAN SEE	WE CAN HEAR
tree	girl
girl	bell
candy	wind
crayon	
bell	

39. Have students pantomime words from their boxes. Class has to guess the word. For example: dog, the student barks; tree, the student stands with arms outstretched, etc.

40. Print sight words that can be illustrated at the bottom of 3 x 5 cards. Make more than one card for each word. Place cards in a box. Students choose cards and draw appropriate pictures. They could put their names on the backs of the cards. Share with the class from time to time as a means of reviewing sight words.

41. Have students look through their words and find a word that means *big*. Have each word read and write it on a chart or on the board. Then have the students decide which word means the "biggest." The words could be synonyms of *big* or they could be words that name big things like an elephant or a whale. Do the same with words that mean *small*. Leave the lists of words on the chart or on the board so that students can add more words.

42. Write service words leaving out one or all vowels. Have students complete the words. (Examples: m__st, __nd.) Words could be in phrases: __n th__ c__r. Lists of service words should be made available. They could be on charts around the room or each student could have a word list.

43. Paste pictures on cards. Prepare short sentences that describe the pictures on other cards. Student matches sentences to pictures and then reads them to someone.

44. Place a large picture on a bulletin board. Prepare word cards to correspond to objects in the picture. Students tack the cards by the appropriate pictures.

45. Give students action sentences and sets of pictures to go with them. Students paste pictures on paper and then write appropriate sentences under pictures.

46. Give students action or descriptive sentences. Have them find pictures in magazines to go with the sentences. The pictures could be cut out and used by other students according to the previous suggestion (activity No. 45)

47. Print common words on cards and place in a box. Have students build sentences with the words. After building each sentence, they should write it on the board or on chart paper.

48. Put incomplete sentences on a chart using service or common words. Sentences like: _____ is small, _____ is bigger than _____, the _____ is on top of the _____. Students use their own word cards to complete the sentences.

49. Print compound words that contain service words on cards. Cut the words apart and put them in an

envelope. The student is to take the cards and make them into compound words. (Examples: cannot, something, everything, sometimes, into, onto, without, inside, outside, another, upon.)

50. Provide students with paper ruled like graph paper and have them make word puzzles by printing service words or words from their boxes in the squares. Have them exchange papers and find each other's words.

PART II
WORD ANALYSIS

WORD ANALYSIS

The immediate problem for students with learning disabilities or severe reading disabilities, is learning and retaining words. Many of these students cannot even write their own names. The response of most classroom teachers is to assume that phonics was never properly taught before and to launch into an intensive phonics program. They soon find that their method of teaching phonics is no more productive or less boring to the student than the years of previous failure. Phonics, like writing one's name, is taught in all schools today beginning in kindergarten. The fact that a student does not "know" phonics is more often a symptom rather than a cause of being unable to read.

Of course phonics is necessary and children acquire phonic skills as part of a total reading program. They learn very quickly, for example, that when reading about someone throwing a ball, the initial consonant *"f"* probably means it was a football, whereas more than the initial consonant *b* is necessary to decide between a baseball and a basketball. Phonics helps them recognize words more quickly and actually enables them to add such words to their sight vocabularies.

Phonics is necessary, but the plea here in introducing these hundred word analysis activities is to go gently with students with learning disabilities. Phonics activities must be related to, actually grow out of, their total reading program. If all they know are a few initial consonant sounds, then begin with those sounds, and let them enjoy success. There are nine activities suggested for initial consonants (Word Analysis 60-68). Students could do all nine with the consonants they know. The confidence they gain will enable them to try something new. We must remember that slow steady progress is better than no progress at all.

The hundred word analysis activities are a combination of phonetic and structural analyses. They are presented in a generally accepted order of difficulty, but not every student learns in this order. In fact, the very first skill, rhyming, is often more difficult for students with learning disabilities than initial consonants and even blends. Some students will be more successful with structural analysis, adding "s" to form plurals, for example, than with phonetic analysis because they can see what they are doing. Learning a word analysis skill should never become an end in itself. A skill is only useful to a student if it helps that student read better. If the student cannot apply the skill, it has no value. Students with learning disabilities often have great difficulty generalizing. They may also become upset to find that a "rule" has an exception. Thus, having never read *come* incorrectly, it suddenly becomes *comb* after the "silent *e* rule" is discussed. Likewise *get* becomes *jet* after learning that "*g*" usually has the "*j*" sound before "*e*" and "*i*". In such instances it's best to forget phonics and teach those words as sight words.

Use the word analysis activities for five to ten minutes a day. Be sure that they are directly related to the reading lesson. From time to time allow the student to review, for being able to do something easier or quicker is a great motivator. Use the word analysis activities in combination with the activities for sight vocabulary, comprehension and vocabulary, and sharing reading.

One test of knowledge is to try to teach someone else. For this reason, the last group of activities are directions for games that students can use to teach others.

51. Cut out pictures that represent rhyming words (mouse, house; rock, sock; for example). Place in an envelope or a box. Have the student match the rhyming pairs.

For added interest, paste a bit of flannel on the backs of the pictures and store them in a flat rectangular box. Paste flannel on the inside of the box lid. The pictures can be matched on the flannel.

This activity can be made self-correcting by putting similar shapes or colors on the backs of matching pairs.

52. Keep a collection of small pictures from old spelling, language, and reading workbooks. Have students search through the pictures to find rhyming pairs. They can be added to the box mentioned in Activity 51.

53. Provide students with pictures of things that rhyme (tree, bee; pail, nail; red, bed; etc.)

They are to make a booklet by pasting two pictures that rhyme on each page. After the booklet is completed, have them look for a third picture for each page.

54. Suggest that students look around the room and outside the window and think of rhymes for the things they see. They could draw pictures of the rhyming objects.

Some examples are: floor, door; mitten, kitten; boy, toy; pen, hen.

55. Have students draw pictures and put five pairs of things in their pictures that rhyme. They could exchange papers and mark the rhyming pairs with different colored crayons. If necessary, draw a picture for the students and tell them to add things to it that rhyme.

56. Make sets of pictures and words that rhyme. Pictures could be: tree, star, cake, cup, fish, horn, hat, skate, spoon, book. Corresponding words could be: see, car, make, up, wish, corn, cat, ate, moon, took. Place them all in a box. Students are to take them out and match them.

57. Print rhyming service words on cards and place them in a box. Students place rhyming words next to each other. This can be made self-checking by putting colored dots on the reverse of the cards.

   Some rhyming service words that could be used are: to, do, two, too, who, blue, you; go, so, no, grow, know, show; be, he, she, me, we, see, three; I, my, by, fly, why, buy, try; may, away, play, today, say.

58. Tell the students to choose a word card and think of something that rhymes with the word. Then find a picture of that thing and paste the picture on paper. Write the rhyming word next to the picture. If the word were *red,* the picture could be *bed.*

   Every classroom should have a box of miscellaneous pictures cut from old spelling, language, math and reading workbooks and from magazines. Students waste too much time when asked to find appropriate pictures in magazines.

59. Cut out pictures that rhyme with service words and are spelled with the same phonograms. The student is to match the words to the pictures and then copy the words and write beside them the names of the pictures. You may have to explain how to do this.

   The service words and the corresponding pictures could be:

at	hat	run	sun	ate	gate	soon	moon
red	bed	see	bee	cut	nut	ten	hen
went	tent	up	cup	five	hive	us	bus
all	ball	did	lid	far	car	wish	fish

big	pig	eat	meat	goes	toes	ask	mask
funny	bunny	get	net	got	pot	best	nest
look	book	may	hay	long	song	how	cow
like	bike	old	gold	pull	bull	keep	jeep
make	cake	saw	paw	read	bead	tell	bell
ran	fan	will	hill	sing	ring	right	light

60. Put one of the following fifteen consonants at the top of a piece of poster paper: b, c, d, f, g, h, j, k, l, m, n, p, r, s, t. Students locate pictures whose names begin with the sound of the consonant and paste them on the poster. Review the sound with individual students by having them identify the pictures.

    Instead of using a poster, make a large letter out of cardboard, and have the pictures pasted on the letter.

61. Have student make a collage by pasting magazine pictures on poster paper. The names of the pictures should all begin with a specified consonant sound. The letter could be placed at the top of the poster or a large letter could be pasted over the collage.

    The collage will look better if the pictures are torn around the edges and pasted so that they overlap.

62. Put two, three or four letters in a box. Add twenty or more pictures of objects whose names begin with the letters. The student is to put the pictures under the appropriate letters.

    Begin with any of the following fifteen initial consonants that the student knows: b, c, d, f, g, h, j, k, l, m, n, p, r, s, t.

63. Have students draw pictures putting in five or as many things as possible that begin with a specified

letter sound.

A "b" picture might contain: book, bag, boy, bat, ball, base, bug, bike.

64. Mount a picture of an object in the center of a large piece of paper. Have students write words they have in their boxes that begin like the object pictured.

65. Provide students with pictures of objects. Under each picture, write the name of the object without the first consonant. Ball, for example, would be written __all. The students are to examine the pictures and supply the missing initial consonants.

   The pictures can be used over and over again if laminated or covered with clear contact paper. The students can write the letters with a felt tip washable marker. They are easily washed with a damp towel. One student can write the letters and a second student can check and erase those that are correct.

66. Copy a chart leaving out initial consonants. Have students write in the missing letters.

   To make this more responsive to individual needs, copy each student's own stories.

67. Remember that one of the best times to teach initial consonants is when a student asks how to spell a word. If the word begins with one initial consonant before a vowel, say, "What letter sound do you hear at the beginning of that word?" (Note: When students ask for words, write them on a piece of scrap paper for them to copy. If you just spell them orally, students will just write the letters without thinking of the whole word.)

68. Challenge students to write sentences in which each word begins with the same letter.
   (Big boys buy big balls.)

69. Place a word on the board or at the top of a chart. As students read or think of other words with the same ending but different beginning consonants, they add them to the chart. Use service words like: ball, ride, sing. If students are not capable of doing this, start with words that do not have an initial consonant like: at, all, and, ate.

70. Put some letters representing ending consonant sounds in a box. Letters would be any of the following: b, d, f, g, l, m, n, p, r, s, t, z. Add pictures of twenty or more objects whose names end with the letters.

    The student is to put the pictures under the appropriate letters. If the letters chosen are m and n, the pictures could be: bone, pen, pin, plane, rain, nine, moon, man, fan, gun, ten, spoon, green, hen, can, home, gum, arm, name, drum, swim, broom, dime, plum.

71. Provide students with pictures of objects. Under each picture, write the name of the object leaving off the last consonant. The students are to examine the pictures and supply the missing ending consonants. Laminate the pictures and have them use felt tip markers.

72. Collect pictures of objects and glue them on cards. Make word cards for each object but print only the first and last letter indicating the middle letters by dashes. Students match pictures and words and then read them to someone.

73. Put five of the following letters on the board: b, d, f, g, l, m, n, p, r, s, t, z. Using their sight vocabulary word cards, students will select one-syllable words ending in the five consonants and write them on another paper, underlining the final consonant for emphasis.

74. Make some "blend" boxes. On the outside of the box, on the lid, print some blends. Use any of the following: bl, cl, fl, gl, pl, sl, sc, sk, sm, sn, sp, st, sw, br, cr, dr, fr, gr, pr, tr.
Put the same blends on cards and place in the box. Then put pictures in the box to represent the blends. Students are to match pictures to appropriate blends.

blue	frog	plane	snake	cradle	sweater
blanket	fruit	plant	snail	crib	swan
block	fraction	plate	snow	cross	swing
skate	scale	spade	brick	train	dragon
ski	scarf	spear	bridge	tree	dress
skirt	school	spider	broom	triangle	drum
glass	grapes	present	slide	clock	flower
glove	green	president	sled	cloud	flag
glue	gray	prune	sleeve	clover	fly
smash	star				
smile	stamp				
smoke	stick				

75. Have students take pictures from magazines where the action represents "blends." Have them indicate the blend. Pictures could represent: driving (dr), sleeping (sl), playing (pl), etc.

76. Have students fold their papers in half, bring the bottom to the top, and then fold in half again from left to right. When opened there will be eight boxes, four on the front and four on the back. Have them look around the classroom for things that begin with a blend. They are to draw the object in one of the boxes and put the blend beside it. Some things might be: plant, block, Brenda, flower.

77. Copy a chart or part of a story leaving out initial consonants and beginning blends. Have students write

in the missing letters. When working with a group, have the students do this and exchange papers.

78. Make up a set of pictures of objects whose names begin with blends. (See 74 for suggestions.) Under each picture, write the name of the object leaving off the initial blend. *Flower,* for example, would be written __ower. Laminate the cards. Students are to write the appropriate blends with a washable felt tip marker.

79. Print words beginning with *k* and *w* on strips of paper. The student is to place paper clips over the letter that gives the initial consonant sound.

    Example: knob king knight knee key knife kick know knot keep knit kite wing wring wrinkle wink wrench wreck wake warm wrap work wrist wish wren west wrong worm wrote water write with

    After doing a number of these, the student could write a "rule" for pronouncing words that begin with wr and kn.

80. Make a set of words ending in *s*. Some will be plurals and some will not, and some will be both. Have the student sort the cards and list them under the three categories.

    Some plurals are: balls, trees, birds, hats, wicks, cabs, kings

    Some that are not plurals: bus, has, goes, yes, his, less, sings

    Some that could be both: calls, bowls, ties, picks, drinks, bats, rings.

81. Choose words from students' word boxes and service words to which *ing* can be added without

changing the root. Have the students write sentences with these words using the models: I am, He is, He was, She is, She was, They are, They were and It is.

Possible words are: go, jump, look, play, see, eat, fall, find, laugh, work, open, pull, read, say, sing, wish, buy, hold, keep, sleep, tell, thank, walk, bring, carry, drink, pick, show, think, wash, call, start.

82. Have available pictures of people doing things like eating, playing, sawing, etc. Make corresponding word cards and have students match the words to the pictures.

83. Cut out ten pictures, mount them on cards and number the cards one to ten. Write twenty sentences leaving one word out of each sentence except its initial consonant. The student is to read the sentences and decide on the basis of the context which words belong in the sentences. This can be indicated by numbering from one to twenty for the sentences and putting the number of the word cards opposite the numbers for the sentences. The first sentence might be:

The boy rode his b_____ to school.

The word (picture) would be bicycle.

Another sentence using the same word could be:

A b_____ has two wheels.

84. Write rhyming elements that are words on cards. Some of these are: age, and, am, an, ate, all, as, at, eat, each, and, is, it, up, in, old. Make a set of consonant cards. The student is to put consonants with the rhyming elements to try to form words. The words should be written on a piece of paper.

85. Make a set of consonant cards and a set of common phonograms. The student forms words with them and makes a list of the words. Some common phonograms are: ack, ad, ail, ake, ank, ark, ash, ay, ell, ent, ick, ight, ing, ock, ot, ug, ump, ung, unk, ush. Some students will need to begin with one or two consonants and one phonogram.

Example: b and r; ack and ake

    back   bake

    rack   rake

After building the words, the student should write them.

86. Put pictures of objects whose names contain short vowel sounds on cards. Under each picture put the name of the object leaving out the vowel. Laminate the cards. Student writes the correct vowel in the blank with a washable felt tip marker.

87. Put pictures of common objects in a box. Choose objects whose names follow a CVC pattern. Some are: hat, bat, cat, rat, bag, pan, fan, cap, jam, hen, pen, ten, red, bed, leg, met, cup, rug, bug, gun, gum, sun, nut, bus, tub, wig, pin, lid, pig, six, mop, pot, box, dog Print the short vowels, a, e, i, o, u, on cards. Make ten of each and put them in the box. The student is to match the short vowels to the appropriate pictures.

88. Using two colors, make vowel and consonant letter cards. Let students experiment to build recognizable words following a CVC pattern. They could make a list of the words.

89. Put small objects (toys) in a box whose names are spelled in CVC pattern. Have the student make word cards for the objects and set them on a table for a display.

Example of toys: pin, pen, car, top, bed, rug, cup, can, dog, cat, hat, rat, etc.

90. Make up a box of fifteen pictures of objects whose names have from one to five or more syllables. Number the pictures. The student is to make a column of numbers from one to fifteen and after the appropriate number write the number of syllables in the name of the object.

    Some pictures and the number of syllables are: clock (1) orange (2) apple (2) refrigerator (5) grasshopper (3) toothbrush (2) basketball (3) violin (3) umbrella (3) pencil (2) truck (1) candlestick (3) thermometer (4) banana (3) pumpkin (2).

    Suggest that students who can do this find five more pictures of objects whose names have three or more syllables, and add them to the box.

91. Have students fold their papers in half the long way and then fold in half again. When unfolded there should be four long boxes. Have them put ack, and, ain, eet at the top of the boxes. Then they are to see how many words they can write beginning with: bl, st, tr, br, pl, sw, sh.

    They could turn the papers over and do the same for oop, ore, ove, ump; and sk, sp, dr, sc, gr, sl.

92. Write a word that begins with a blend and ends with a common phonogram at the top of a narrow piece of paper. The student is to locate other words that have the same phonogram but different blends and write them under the original word. Some words to use are black, train, snake, plate, stay, dream, stick, bring, clock.

    If the word were *black*, some expected responses would be: crack, flack, shack, stack, slacks, smack, snack, track.

93. Make a set of blend cards using some or all of the following: bl, cl, fl, gl, pl, sl, sc, sk, sm, sn, sp, st, sw, br, cr, dr, fr, gr, pr, tr.

    Then make a set of phonogram cards. Some phonograms are: ace, ack, ad, ade, ail, ain, ake, ale, ame, amp, ank, ap, ark, art, ash, ay; eam, ean, ear, eck, eep, ell, end, est, ick, ight, ike, ill, ind, ine, ing, ink, int, ip, irt; oach, oat, ock, oil, oke, old, ong, op, ore, ot, ought, ound; ub, uck, ug, um, ump, unch, ung, unk, unt, ush, ust.

    Put all in a box. The student is to form words with the blends and phonograms and write them on a piece of paper. The choices for this activity will have to be limited for those with severe reading disabilities. Start, for example, with bl, br, cr, fl, sh, sm, sn, st, tr and ack, ake, amp, ank, ock.

94. Put pictures on cards to represent the following ending blends: ft, nt, rt, rd, rk, st. Pictures could be: raft, gift, plant, ant, cent, tent, fort, sport, skirt, shirt, card, board, pork, fork, cork, toast, chest, ghost, nest.

    Under each picture write the name of the object, but leave off the ending blend. Laminate the cards. The student is to write the blends with a washable felt tip marker. Another student can read them and erase, i.e. wash off, those that are correct.

95. Put a word or phrase related to a holiday, season, or school event at the top of a piece of chart paper. Have students make words with the letters and write them on the chart paper.

96. Have students contribute to long vowel posters or collages. Focus on one vowel at a time. They cut out pictures of objects whose names contain that long vowel sound and paste them on the poster or col-

lage. The vowel letter in different type and color cut from magazine ads could be part of the collage.

97. Make a "bingo" card. Put a picture in each square. Provide words with the same vowel sounds as those in the pictures. Students place word cards over proper pictures. Since the student is matching vowel sounds, the pictures and words will not be the same. The word *but* could be matched to a picture of a cup.

98. Make up a box of one-syllable service words that have short and long vowel sounds. Place sufficient cards containing "breves" (˘) and "macrons" (-) in the box. The student is to place a (˘) over a short vowel and a (-) over a long vowel. Words could be: am an at big come help jump red did black have some stop yes cut give go he I like make me play see we be came find may no she ate five made pay gave grow hold keep kind sleep take white both clean don't know right show those write light six ten us wish best from much must tell think with well done drink pick them then think went but.

99. Give students columns from a newspaper and have them find examples of vowel sounds.

    Find five short 'e' vowels and color them red. Color five long 'e' vowels green.

100. Give students ten short sentences omitting all vowels. Have them rewrite them providing the vowels.

    Wh-t t-m- -s -t? would be rewritten,

    What time is it?

101. Many students with learning disabilities are not very flexible. They find it difficult to accept the idea that there can be exceptions to "rules." Therefore, before

beginning work on the vowel generalization involving the final *e*, be sure to review the exceptions that are already in the student's sight vocabulary. Have the student sort them into two piles labeled long vowel sounds and short sounds, ask, "In what way do all the words look alike?"

Put the following words on cards:

love	come	are	like	five	these
done	some	one	make	made	those
gone	have	were	ride	gave	write
none	give	there	came	take	
			ate	white	

102. Put the following words, or other similar ones, on cards:

hat	fin	hate	fine
kit	ton	kite	tone
hid	bit	hide	bite
rod	not	rode	note
cut	mat	cute	mate
rid	mad	ride	made
pin	win	pine	wine
rip	rob	ripe	robe
tap	cub	tape	cube
fat	rat	fate	rate

The student is to sort the cards into two piles: long vowel sounds and short vowel sounds. The student then writes two "rules."One rule for the words with short vowel sounds and one for the words with long vowel sounds.

103. Give students columns from newspapers. Have them find words that follow the --VCe pattern and write them in two columns: short vowel words and long vowel words.

104. Make the following phrases and contractions: I am, I will, is not, did not, do not, it is, she is, he is, what is, can not; I'm, I'll, isn't, didn't, don't, it's, she's, he's, what's, can't.

The student is to match the contractions to the phrases.

105. Make the following word cards: am, will, did, do, it, she, he, what, can. Also make two cards for *I*, two for *am*, five for *is* and six for *not*.

Then make four of each of the following letters: a, c, d, e, h, l, m, n, and w. In addition, make eight of 'i', 6 of 's', 6 of 't', 5 of 'o', and 10 of '.

Put them in a box with the following phrases: I am, I will, is not, did not, do not, it is, she is, he is, what is, can not.

First the student is to use the word cards to make the phrases. Then use the letter cards to make the phrases. The student then removes the letters necessary to make the contraction, puts the letters to one side and rebuilds the contraction using the apostrophe cards.

| I am | I'm | a |
| I will | I'll | wi |

106. Make a "bingo" card with nine squares. Put the following contractions in the squares: I'm, isn't, didn't, don't, it's, she's, he's, what's, can't. Make fifteen little squares. Put *o*'s on five of them, *a*'s on five and *i*'s on five. The student is to cover the contraction with the missing letter. *I'm*, for example, would be covered by *a*, *isn't* would be covered by *o*.

107. Mount pictures of objects whose names begin with ch and sh. Under each picture put the name of the object without the beginning digraph. Indicate that with two dashes (Ship would be written --ip.).

Laminate the cards. The students write in the missing digraphs with a washable felt tip marker. Pictures could be: ship, shirt, sheep, shell, shoe, shovel, shark, shed, shelf, shoulder, church, chair, chicken, chimney, chalk, child, children, chain, checker, cheese, chipmunk, check.

108. Provide the student with a box of pictures cut from old spelling, reading, and language workbooks and from magazines and other sources. Also give the student four cards on which are printed ch, sh, th, wh. The student is to locate pictures whose names begin with those sounds.

109. Make a list of words containing initial consonant digraphs. Leave off the digraphs. Have students determine what the words are by definition and fill in the missing letters.
    --ip   It goes on water.
    --air   You sit in it.
    --ip   A little piece of wood.

110. Mount pictures of objects whose names end with the consonant digraphs ck, ch, sh, ng, nk, and th. Pictures could be: duck, stick, sock, block, truck; peach, church, inch, sandwich, ranch; fish, dish, brush, cash, wash; ring, king, song, wing, ping pong; pink, tank, sink, link, trunk; path, cloth, wreath, teeth, tooth. Under each picture write the name leaving off the ending digraph (du--, sti--, etc.). Laminate them. The student is to fill in the missing digraphs with a washable felt tip marker.

111. Make a list of words containing final consonant digraphs and their definitions. Leave off the digraphs. Have students determine what the words are by the definitions and write the words on a separate piece of paper opposite the appropriate numbers.

lo —	On a door	si —	Make music
tor —	You light it	i —	You write with it
ru —	In a hurry	bo —	Two

112. Using words similar to the pictures of Activity #110 above, have the student choose a word card, draw a picture to illustrate the word, and then write the word under the picture.

113. Students with reading disabilities tend to have difficulty with words containing er, ir and ur. They handle the difficulty by reversing the letters so bird, for example, becomes brid. Give students pictures of objects whose names contain er, ir and ur. Put the names of the objects on other cards and have them matched. Pictures and words could be: bird, girl, shirt, skirt, fern, curl, fur, church, berth, purse.

114. Have students look through the classroom collection of magazine pictures to find people doing things. They write what they are doing on a card and paste it on the picture. They have to decide the correct spelling when *ing* is added.

115. Make up a box of pictures of objects whose names contain the dipthongs ou ow (as in cow), oi and oy. Add other pictures to represent long and short o and a sounds. On a sufficient number of little cards write ou, ow, oi, oy, ā, ă, ō, and ŏ. The student matches the sounds to the pictures. Note that at this time the student is not expected to know whether or not a word is spelled with oi or oy and ou or ow so both sets of these cards should be on such words unless the student does know. Pictures might be: boy, toy, coin, oil, cow, owl, house, cloud, clown, ouch, gown, brown, towel, flower, mouse, snow, crow, soap, coat, pony, frog, box, map.

116. The vowel digraph *ea* is prounounced many ways. Most words will have the long *e* sound as in *eat.* Many words in beginning reading materials have long *e*, but controlled by *r* as in *year*. This slight difference can be confusing to a student with a learning disability. The second most frequent pronunciation is short *e* as in *head.* Beginning readers will see many two syllable words with short *e* as *pleasant*. In a few words *ea* has a long *a* sound as in *great*.

Students need to be willing to be flexible when pronouncing words containing *ea.* Tell them that the following words (on word cards) are all words they have heard. They are to try pronouncing them until they are sure of the word. Begin with a long *e*, then, if necessary, try a short *e*, then a long *a*. Put the words in three (or if you want to treat *ear* differently), or four columns.

Four columns would look like this:

eat	ear	head	great
tea	dear	dead	break
sea	hear	deaf	steak
flea	near	bread	
each	year	feather	
east	clear	ready	
speak	spear	instead	
real		meadow	
team		pleasant	
teach		breakfast	

117. The vowel digraph *ea* is usually pronounced three ways: long *e* as in *eat*, short *e* as in *thread*, and long *a* as in *steak*. (Note that some words have two pronunciations: read, lead, tear, and that some are exceptions such as heart and early.)

Have students find examples of the three usual pronunciations and write phrases with them.

great steak
clean break
dead flea
neat team
screaming eagle

118. Students have had practice making plurals by adding *s* when the root does not change. (See Activity #80). They need to be aware of structural changes in the root when a word ends in *y*. To make a plural when a word ends in *y*, change the *y* to *i* and add *es*. Using these words: baby, puppy, candy, cooky, family, city, have students complete the following phrases:

two _____
one _____
many _____
each _____
a _____
a few _____
some _____

Note that *some* can be used both with the singular and plural forms of some words such as candy and family.

119. After mastering common blends, some students fail to note three-letter blends. To bring awareness, have them illustrate and label, by copying, the following words: ring, sting, string, spring; lash (eye), sash, splash; trap, strap; rip, trip, strip; truck, struck.

Have them look in books for other words with three-letter blends. Some words they might find are: scrabble, scramble, scrap, scrape, scratch, scream, screech, screen, screw, scribble, scrub; straight, strange, stranger, strangle, strap, straw, strawberry, stream, street, strength, stretcher, strict, strike, stripe, stroke, strong, struck, struggle; spray, spread, sprinkle, spruce; square, squash, squeak, squeal, squeeze, squirrel.

120. Students will probably come upon more words where oo is pronounced as in *too*, the long sound, than as in *book*, the short sound. Use the following sight words, plus any other words they want to add: book, brook, food, foot, good, look, moon, noon, room, soon, too, took, zoo, zoom. Have them put the words into two columns according to the pronunciation of *oo*. Then they are to find other words to add to their lists. Do all words go in one or the other lists? What about door, floor, and blood? What is a good rule to follow when pronouncing words containing two *o*'s together? (Try long sound as in *too*, first.)

Some other words are: tooth, root, broom, loose, moose, loop, hoop, scoop, boot, cool, tool, pool, spool, spoon, roof and hook, wood, wool, cook, shook, stood.

121. Have students make two-word phrases with words that contain double *oo*'s.
Example: loose tooth
good book
cool food
good food
look good
look cool
cool brook
They could be two types, those where the *o*'s are pronounced the same and those where the *o*'s are pronounced differently.

122. Make up four boxes of words to illustrate each of the four vowel principles. Put a vowel principle on the in-

side lid of a box. Put words that follow the principle and words that are exceptions on cards and place them in the box. The students are to sort the words into the two categories. (This can be made self-checking by marking the backs of the word cards.) To add interest, make the boxes and cards colorful.

Box 1: On the outside of the lid, put in large letters, CVC.

On the inside of the lid, put, "When there is one vowel between two consonants, the vowel sound is usually short."

Since most CVC words follow this "rule" there will be no difficulty finding words. Some exceptions are: hold, told, dark, far, jar, star, fall, farm, for, kind, most, talk, word, warm, part, work, turn.

Box 2: On the outside of the lid, put in large letters, CV.

On the inside of the lid, put, "When there is one vowel at the end of a word following a consonant, the vowel sound is usually long."

(Note that this "rule" will be more important later when applied to syllables.)

Words could be: be, he, me, she, we, go, no, so, by, my, cry, dry, fly, sky. Some exceptions are: do, to, ski, ha, ma, pa.

Box 3: On the outside of the lid, put in large letters, CVVC.

On the inside of the lid, put "When there are two vowels between two consonants, the first vowel sound is usually long and the second vowel is usually silent."

There are so many exceptions that this is a questionable "rule." *ee* and *oa* have fewer exceptions than other combinations.

Words with ee: feet, keep, seen, need, week
Words with oa: boat, soak, toast, soap, road
Words with ai: rain, wait, paid, mail, pain
Words with ea: bean, leaf, seat, dream, meal

Exceptions: Joanne, hair, chair, said, head, heard, pleasant, bread, deaf, ready, feather, sweater, great, steak, break, true, blue, glue, vein, ceiling, sleigh, chief, field, your, would.

Box 4: On the outside of the lid, put in large letters, VCe. On the inside of the lid, put, "When a word ends in *e,* the preceding vowel is usually long."

Exceptions are: above, are, before, care, come, done, eye, give, gone, have, love, minute, move, none, one, office, scare, some, sure, there, were, where, whose. Words that look somewhat similar but follow the "rule": alone, ate, bite, brave, cage, cake, came. drove, face, five, shone, game, gave, home, late, made, nine, ride, save, shone, same, stone, take, these, those, tire, wave.

123. Divide a large sheet of paper into four columns and at the top of each column write abbreviations for the four vowel principles.

CVC (One vowel between two consonants — vowel sound is usually short)

CV (One vowel following a consonant — vowel sound is usually long)

CVVC (Two vowels between two consonants — the first vowel sound is usually long and the second vowel is usually silent.)

CVCe (The final *e* is silent, and the preceding vowel is long)

Provide the students with newspaper headlines and advertisements, pages from magazines and other appropriate sources of words. Have them locate words that illustrate the four vowel principles, cut them out and paste them in the appropriate columns on the chart.

124. Write each of the vowel principles, or their abbreviations, on a chart. (See Activity #123 above.) Under the generalization, make two columns labeled, "Follows the rule" and "Does not follow the rule." Students are to find examples as they read and write the words in appropriate columns.

125. Make the following phrases and contractions: We will, she will, they will, you will, will not, we are, you are, they are, could not, I have, she would, he would, they would; we'll, she'll, they'll, you'll, won't, we're, you're, they're, couldn't, I've, she'd, he'd, they'd.

    The student is to match the contractions to the phrases.

126. Make up a box of words, letters, and apostrophes. You will need a minimum of the following: they $-$ 6, will $-$ 5, we $-$ 4, she $-$ 4, you $-$ 4, are $-$ 3, would $-$ 3, not $-$ 2, could $-$ 2, I $-$ 2, he $-$ 2, have $-$ 1; and I $-$ 8, e $-$ 4, d $-$ 3, r $-$ 3, n $-$ 2, t $-$ 2, o $-$ 1, v $-$ 1, w $-$ 1, and 13 apostrophes ('). Put them in a box with the following phrases: we will, she will, they will, you will, will not, we are, you are, they are, could not, I have, she would, he would, they would.

    First the student is to use the word cards to make the phrases. Then use the rest of the word cards and the letters to make the phrases. The student then removes the letters necessary to make the contraction, puts the letters to one side and rebuilds the contraction using the apostrophe cards.

we will	we'll	wi
she will	she'll	wi

127. Some students have difficulty with words ending in *ed*. There are "rules" for verbs:

When a verb ends in *d* or *t* before adding *ed*, the *ed* is pronounced like *ed* in bed. Examples: added, landed, needed, ended, loaded, started, waited, lasted, hunted, skated.

When a verb ends in a voiced consonant or a vowel sound before adding *ed*, the *ed* is pronounced like a *d*. Examples: spelled, seemed, farmed, begged, lived, played, sighed, tied, freed, mowed.

When a verb ends in an unvoiced consonant sound before adding *ed*, the *ed* is pronounced like a 't'. Examples: looked, walked, jumped, asked, hatched, laughed, kissed, wished, stamped, rocked.

Students could be given the three "rules" and the words on cards to be placed under the "rules."

128. Give students a list of words that require the last consonant to be doubled before adding *ing, y, er,* and *est*. These will be mostly CVC words. The consonant has to be doubled so that the vowel sound will remain short. Have them add any of the endings to make new words.

Possible words are: run, plan, big, fun, cut, dig, fat, sun, glad, grin, hot, put, red, rub, sad, fur, bat, bet, bud, cab, dog, tip, wag, wet, win, stop.

129. Print "Hard C" on one card and "Soft C" on another. Put in an envelope with the following words: call, cedar, circle, candle, candy, celery, cycle, come, came, cut, cake, city, center, cent, circus, could, cold, ice, become, face, fact, space, mice, princess, pencil, fence, since, raccoon, clock, because, coin.

Students decide whether the *c*'s are "hard" or "soft" according to the "rule." When *c* is followed by *e, i,* or *y,* it has the "soft" or *s* sound, otherwise it has the "hard" or *k* sound.

130. Print "Hard G" on one card and "Soft G" on another. Put in an envelope with the following words: gate, go, garden, gave, got, gold, guess, glad, glue, good, gulf, gum; gem, gym, gip, giraffe, geranium, germ, general, gently, giant, ginger, gypsy, age; give, get, girl, gift, giggle, gear, gill, girdle, gizzard.

Students sort the words into three piles: "Hard G" and "Soft G" and follow the rule, and a third pile for words that do not follow the "rule." The "rule" is, when g is followed by e, i, or y it usually has the "soft" or j sound, otherwise it has the "hard" or g sound.

131. Provide students with advertisements, lists of sight words, and material that they can read, and have them find five "hard c" words, five "soft c" words, five "hard g" words that follow the rule, five "soft g" words that follow the rule, and as many other words containing a g that do not follow the rule, as they can.

132. Give students the following models or similar ones:

They _____ again.   He did not _____ right.
They will _____.   He will need to _____.

Have them make sensible sentences using the following words as they are and with the prefix re meaning again: run, cross, build, write, call, count, enter, join, learn, and teach.

She is not_____.   It is not _____.
She is _____.   It is _____.

For the above, use the following words as they are and with the prefix un meaning not: able, afraid, changed, cooked, covered, cut, done, happy, loved, open, packed, real, safe, sold, true, wise.

133. The simplest suffixes often have many different shades of meaning. *Ful*, for example, means "full of" in words like *careful, joyful* and *thoughtful*, but it has a slightly different meaning in *spoonful* and *harmful*. Therefore, rather than attempt to teach all the meanings, make learning disabled students aware that many long words that may look difficult to them are really words they know with prefixes and suffixes added.

Make a box of prefixes, suffixes, and root words and have students build words and write them to be checked.

Prefixes: re, un, in, dis, con, pre

Suffixes: ful, less, ment, ness, able, tion, sion

Root words: care, joy, spoon, harm, thought, agree, color, finish, home, count, believe, fill, pay, cancel, caution.

134. Have students take words from their word boxes that have two syllables and have double consonants in the middle. Because the words are from their boxes, they will all be words they know. If you prefer, use the following sight words which students should know before doing this activity: better, bunny, butter, daddy, dinner, dollar, follow, funny, happy, jelly, kitten, letter, matter, penny, puppet, puppy, rabbit, squirrel, summer, supper, village, yellow, zipper. They are to write the words in a column, making a chart. After each word, state how many syllables are in the word (two). Then state what vowel sound is heard in the first syllable (All will be short vowels.) With what letter does the first syllable have to end to keep the vowel short? (All will be one of the double letters.) Go back to the word in the first column and draw a line after that letter. Where were all the words divided? (Between the double consonants.) Now write a "rule" for dividing words into syllables when the word has double consonants. When there

are two like consonants in a word, divide between those two consonants.

bet/ter	2	short e	t	between the two *t*'s
bun/ny	2	short u	n	between the two *n*'s

Look in a book for words that are new to you that follow this "rule." Find five new words and add them to your chart.

135. Have the students make a chart like the one above (Activity #134) for the following sight words: after, also, garden, gerbil, into, Monday, number, party, pencil, picture, sister, Sunday, under, until, and winter.

The "rule" will now be: When two consonants come between two vowels, divide between the two consonants.

af/ter	2	short a	f	between f and t
gar/den	2	a controlled by r	r	between r and d
pen/cil	2	short e	n	between n and c

Look in a book for five words new to you that follow this "rule," and add them to your chart.

136. Suggest that students take words from their boxes that end with a consonant followed by *le* or use the following sight words: apple, bottle, candle, cattle, circle, handle, kettle, little, middle, people, puddle, purple, riddle, table, uncle. Note that students will be working with words they know. They are to divide them into syllables and note which letter begins the last syllable. They could make a chart:

ap/ple	p
bot/tle	t
can/dle	d

Then they are to write a "rule" for words where the last syllable ends in *le*. "When the last syllables of a word ends in *le*, the consonant before the *le* usually begins the last syllable." Then they are to find five new words that follow this "rule" and add them to their charts.

137. Have students pronounce the following sight words: baby, begin, lady, music, open, over, paper, zebra. What did they notice about the vowel sound in the first syllable? (It was long.) Look at the next two letters. Are they vowels or consonants? What is the pattern in each word? (VCV) Write a syllabication "rule" for such words. "When there is one consonant between two vowels, the word is usually divided after the first vowel." Have the students find five words that follow this "rule." Find words that do not follow the "rule." There are many. (oven, seven, holiday, very, camel)

138. Tell the students that when dividing words into syllables, ch, sh, th, wh, and most blends are not divided. Show them a few examples like teach/er, se/cret, sur/prises, broth/er. Have them find five words, underline the digraph or blend and then divide them using the "rules" they know. They may discover some exceptions like *st* (mas/ter) and *sp* (whis/per).

139. Return to Activity #133 (Prefixes, Suffixes, and Roots). This time have students divide the words into syllables noting that prefixes and suffixes usually form separate syllables. Other words to use: disagreement, unkindness, renewable, distasteful, disrespectful, prepayment, unpleasantness, unskillful, readjustment, indirectness, unsuccessful, untuneful, redevelopment, undrinkable, unharmful, unhelpful, unfairness.

140. The purpose of vowel and syllabication "rules" is to help students pronounce unknown words when they are reading. First, they should always read to the end of the sentence and try to get a context clue. Then they can check the word against their knowledge of phonics. Failing this, they have to look in a dictionary and this is so time consuming that most students won't do it. Help them learn a systematic way of figuring out words.

Provide them with words of three, four or more syllables that they probably don't know. Using their knowledge of vowel "rules" they are to determine the number of vowel *sounds* in each word. This is a clue to the number of syllables. Then they are to use their knowledge of syllabication principles to divide the words into syllables and pronounce them. The dictionary will be the final authority. Some possible words:

in/for/ma/tion/
ar/gu/ment
as/tro/naut
mo/men/tum
non/re/stric/tive
pas/sen/ger
pro/vin/cial/ism
au/to/graph
sea/man/ship
trem/u/lous
un/com/plain/ing
whip/per/snap/per
re/fine/ment
pug/na/cious

141. Being able to teach something to someone else is the real test of knowledge. Just making an activity to do this is a learning experience in itself. This and the following activities through #150 will be specific instructions for making reading games to be made

by and used by students to teach other students. The first is RHYMING CONCENTRATION. Like all the games, it can be adapted to teach other reading skills. Suggestions will be made for INITIAL CONSO-NANT CONCENTRATION, FINAL CONSONANT CONCENTRATION and INITIAL BLEND CONCEN-TRATION.

First, nearly everyone knows how to play concentra-tion. We will use sixteen cards. Shuffle the cards and place them face down in rows. The first player turns over any two cards. If they match, the player keeps them and turns over two more cards. If they don't match, the cards are placed face down again leaving them in the same place. The next player takes a chance. When all the cards are paired the game is over. The winner is the player with the most pairs.

To make the rhyming cards: Cut sixteen cards out of oaktag or use old playing cards. Find eight pairs of pictures of things that represent eight different rhyming words and glue them to the cards. They could be:

            boy - toy
            pail - sail
            mop - top
            cat - hat
            light - kite
            book - hook
            pen - ten
            red - bed

Pictures for INITIAL CONSONANT game could be:

    b: bird - bee
    d: dog - dime
    g: gum - goose
    p: pail - pin
    m: moon - mouse
    n: nuts - nail
    r: rose - red
    s: sun - six

Pictures for FINAL CONSONANT game could be:
- t: boat - cat
- d: sled - hand
- n: pen - fan
- r: chair - car
- b: bib - web
- g: rug - bag
- p: top - lamp
- l: ball - hill

Pictures for the INITIAL BLEND game could be:
- bl: block - blue
- cr: cracker - crow
- dr: dress - drum
- tr: truck - tree
- fl: flag - fly
- cl: cloud - clock
- pl: plant - plate
- fr: frog - freezer

142. INITIAL CONSONANT GAME.

To make the game: Choose five different consonant sounds, and find four pictures of things that begin with each of the sounds. You could have:
- d: duck, dog, desk, doll
- b: book, boy, bike, bell
- t: top, two, tiger, turtle
- s: saw, sail, soap, sun
- m: moon, man, mop, mouse

Paste the pictures on colored oaktag cut into squares. To play the game: Mix the cards up and put them in a box or in an envelope. Get a friend to time you. Dump the pictures on a table and see how fast you can put them in five lines so that all the pictures in each line begin with the same sound. Then let your friend try to beat you. Take the cards to a first or second grade and teach some children there how to play. See if you can teach them so well that they can do it in less time than it took you the first time you tried it.

143. LETTER SOUNDS.

To make the game: Paste pictures on cards to represent each letter of the alphabet. You might have an apple for *a,* a box for *b,* a car for *c,* etc. To play the game: Take the cards to a first grade. Shuffle the cards and show them one at a time to a child. The child is to tell you what the first letter would be. (Sometimes the child might have the correct sound, but the wrong letter like *k* for *c* in car. This would have to be called correct if you are asking for the *sounds* of the letter.) The child keeps each card that is said correctly. You get those that are missed. The person with the most cards wins. Remember that you want the child to win!

144. INITIAL CONSONANTS SOUNDS BLOCK TOSS.

To make the game: Make a cube out of oaktag or use a wooden block. Find six pictures of things that begin with six *different* consonant sounds and paste them on the six sides of the cube. Be sure that each word begins with only one consonant followed by a vowel. Some pictures you might have are:

d: duck	v: valentine	s: sun
b: boy	f: fan	m: milk
g: girl	j: jug	n: nail
h: hand	k: kitten	p: pencil
t: top	l: lamp	r: rose

To play the game: Toss the block. Name the picture on the top. Then give a word that begins with the same sound as the name of the picture. Take turns. Keep score by putting markers (beans, buttons, bottle caps, pieces of paper) in front of the players. To get a marker, a player must give a word with the correct sound. No one can repeat a word given by another player. Play for ten minutes. The player with the most markers at the end of the time wins.

145. VOWEL CARD GAME.

To make the game: Make a list of words to illustrate the long and short vowels. Have three words for each vowel sound. You will have thirty cards which will be enough for two players. Examples of long *a* words: rain, hay, bake.

To play the game: Shuffle the cards and give each player five cards. Put the rest in a pile face down in the center of a table. Take the top card off the pile and place it next to the pile, face up. This will be the discard pile. The players begin the game by looking at the five cards in their hands to see if three of them have the same vowel sounds. If they do, the player reads the three words aloud, and if the other player agrees, the cards are placed on the table and that player has a "book." No player can hold more than five cards at one time so when a player has more than five cards, that player must put one face up on the discard pile. The player with the most "books" wins. You could play this game with one other person or you could teach two people to play it.

146. SYLLABLE CARD GAME FOR TWO PLAYERS.

To make the game: Get thirty pictures and paste each picture on a card. Use pictures of things that have lots of syllables in their names like butterfly, refrigerator, watermelon.

To play the game: Shuffle the cards and place them face down in the middle of the table. The first player takes the top card, names the picture and tells how many syllables are in the name. If correct, the card is placed on the table face up. If not correct, the card is placed on the bottom of the pile in the center of the table. The second player then takes the top card and does the same thing. As soon as both players have cards, the player with the card with the most number of syllables takes both cards to keep. If there are the same number of syllables on both cards, the cards should be placed back into any part of the pile. The player with the most cards wins.

147. QUESTIONS AND ANSWERS — A CARD GAME.

To make the game: Make up twenty questions about reading skills that you think a second grader could answer. Examples — What are two words that rhyme with *green*? What word with a long vowel sound is the name of a very large plant? (tree) Put the questions and the answers on cards.

To play the game: Take the game to two second graders. Shuffle the cards and put them in a pile face down in the middle of a table. One player takes the top card and reads the question to the other player who must answer it. If the answer is correct, that player gets the card. If the answer is not correct, the person who reads the question keeps the card. Have the players take turns. The player with the most cards wins. Shuffle the cards and have them play the game two more times. Your job is to see that they play correctly. Were there any questions that they both couldn't answer? Talk about these questions with them and teach them the answers.

148. PHONICS GAME.

To make the game: Make a game board and put statements about phonics in most of the sections. Examples: Say two words that begin with *b*. Give a word that ends in *d*. Say three words that rhyme with *boat*. Put other statements in, too. Examples: Go back two spaces. Move to the picture of _____.
Make a set of cards with numbers on them. Make five cards for each number from one to six. There will be thirty cards all together. Make some markers.

To play the game: Shuffle the cards and place them in a pile face down in the middle of the table or on a special place on the game board. A player takes the top card and moves a marker the same number of spaces as the number on the card. Then the player must do what it says in the space. If the player can't do it, the marker must be moved back to the original space. You could play this game with someone or you could teach two people to play it.

149. VOWEL GAME.

To make the game: Make a game board and decide on a theme for the game. It could be rockets going to the moon, horses racing, or some other theme. Make a list of words related to the theme that have long or short vowels in them. Example: If the theme is rockets going to the moon, some of the words could be: cone, sky, pad, space, blast. You can also use other words if you can't think of words related to the theme. Put one word in each space on the game board. Make some pictures to use for markers (astronauts, for example). Then make the following cards: three that say "long *a* sound," three that say "short *a* sound" and continue with three cards for all the other vowels — long and short *e*, long and short *i*, long and short *o*, and long and short *u*. You will have thirty cards.

To play the game: Shuffle the cards. Place them in a pile face down in the middle of the table. Each player takes a card and moves a marker to the first word that has the same vowel sound as the card. If there are no more, the player can't move. The players take turns, and the first player to get to the end wins.

150. SENTENCE READING

To make the game: Make a game board and decorate it to fit a theme or a book. Then put short sentences and game directions on cards. Example: Theme — Horse Racing. One card could read:

The horse can jump high
Move two spaces.

Make some markers (horses, for example). If you use a book, you can take words and sentences from the book.

To play the game: Shuffle the cards and place them in a pile face down in the middle of the table. Each player takes a card. If the player can't read it, the player moves backwards. After the cards are picked, they should be placed at the bottom of the pile. The player to reach the end first wins.

Since you made this game, you will be able to read all the sentences. Take the game to two or three children and teach them how to play it. Your job is to make sure that they read the sentences correctly.

PART III
COMPREHENSION
AND
VOCABULARY

COMPREHENSION
AND
VOCABULARY

Comprehension is more than a series of skills. Learning to note details, to identify a sequence of events, and even to recognize the main idea will not insure understanding of a selection. Reading is thinking and just as there are different levels of thinking, there are different levels of comprehending what one reads. Whether or not it is necessary to teach "comprehension" and whether or not it can be taught are often debated, but those of us who work with students with learning disabilities know that it is necessary and that it can be done. The most common strategy is to engage students in discussion guided by questions. This is very important, but it assumes that students have acquired the concepts and vocabulary necessary for the discussion. Since most students with severe reading disabilities have not acquired them, some of the following hundred classroom activities address this problem. There are activities to develop listening and reading vocabularies, to understand relationships and think in abstract terms, to classify and categorize, to appreciate adjectives, to understand pronouns, idioms and prepositional and adverbial phrases, and to become aware of homonyms, synonyms, and antonyms.

The second type include activities that focus on the organization of the reading material itself. These include developing awareness of words that signal sequences, increasing attention to details, understanding the uses of punctuation, making use of illustrations, understanding the interrelationship of sentences, using the context to recognize and understand the meaning of words, locating the main idea, and making use of summary statements.

The third type include activities directed toward making students aware of techniques that they can use to improve their understanding and memory. Using mental imagery is one example. Poor readers seldom have any mental images when they read. They don't *see* the swallows flying in and out of Mr. Zuckerman's barn. They don't *hear* the whippoorwill across the road. They don't *smell* the smoke from Lurvy's pipe. They don't *hear* the tree toad or the slamming of the kitchen door. They don't *feel* comfortable and happy so they don't *experience* the fear that makes Wilbur tremble when he remembers what the old sheep had told him. If they did have these mental pictures, they would understand and remember. Another example is making inferences. Good readers automatically infer action and elaborate on settings. This skill can be developed. Students can also help themselves by asking themselves questions and thus, setting purposes as they read.

These hundred *Comprehension and Vocabulary* activities are intended to supplement the reading lesson. They require students to think, and most of the activities offer concrete experiences with words, phrases, and sentences. The order of difficulty is based on reading and writing ability rather than on a taxonomy of thinking or reading comprehension. Thus, in one of the early activities on "inferences," (#156) students draw pictures to indicate the solution to riddles. In a later activity on "inferences," (#231), they are expected to be reading books and after each chapter writing answers to: "Tell one thing that happened. Why did it happen?" and "Tell one thing that somebody did. Why did they do it?"

So that teachers will know the objective of each activitiy, they have short labels such as, Vocabulary, Imagery, Classification, Inferences, Sequence, Phrases, Details, Pronouns, Main Idea, and Summaries.

151. Vocabulary: To increase listening vocabulary, have students choose a new word to learn each day. Everyone tries to use the word as many times as possible during the day. Some students might take the word home so that their families could use it, too.

152. Imagery: Many students who can read words, but do not comprehend, make no attempt to visualize a story. They have to be shown how to do this. Begin with one word such as *ball*. Everyone draws a picture of a ball and writes a sentence describing a ball. Why are all the pictures and sentences different?

153. Classification: Place a cardboard divider in a shoe box to make two sections. Label the sections "kitchen" and "living room" or "summer" and "winter" or other categories. Provide appropriate pictures. Students place pictures in the correct sections.

154. Classification: Divide a large sheet of paper into four sections. Label them kitchen, bedroom, living room, and bath. Have students cut out pictures and words from magazines and paste them in the appropriate sections.

155. Classification: Paste a picture of a boy or girl at the top of a large sheet of paper. Students find pictures of things to go with them. Pictures could come from catalogs and magazines. (Clothing, things to do, things to play with, etc.)

156. Inference: Write "riddles." Students show the solution by drawing pictures. Examples:

It is big.	It can fly.
It is brown.	It is blue.
It wags its tail.	It calls, "Jay, Jay."
It is a pet.	

It is round.
It is flat.
It looks like a plate.
Boys and girls throw it.
After students can do this, they could make up riddles themselves.

157. Classification: Make shape books. Cut pages into shapes (house, car, animal, circle, square, etc.) Students find pictures and paste them in the appropriate books. Circle books could have pictures of coins, plates, pies, cakes, clocks, rings, etc.

158. Classification: Choose a category such as *toys* or *things to ride*, etc. Have students find words in their word boxes that would fit the category. They could make lists and read them to each other.

159. Sequence: Cook something, make cookies or ice cream, do a science experiment or perform a magic trick. Then have the students dictate a chart about it to show the steps in sequence.

160. Vocabulary: Place a sentence on a chart or on the board with a descriptive word omitted. Students list words that would make sense.

See the _____ apple.
red
big
rotten
etc.

The same could be done for verbs.
The boy _____ the boat.
sailed
saw
painted
anchored
built

161. Following directions: Write directions for placing pictures on an individual flannel board. One student carries out the directions. Then another student checks. Example:

> Put a red house in the middle.
> Put a yellow duck by the house.
> Put three more ducks on the other side of the house.

162. Classification: Choose a topic like flowers, birds, fish, clothing, etc. Suggest that students browse in picture dictionaries to find examples. When they do they write the word on a chart with a brief description.

163. Phrases: Make a box or an envelope of simple pictures and write phrases or short sentences for each. Students are to match phrases to pictures. Examples:

on the floor	See the dog.
in the bed	The ball is red.
around the house	A boy is skating.
chasing a ball	on a bicycle
in the house	over the tree

164. Main Idea: Choose an old chart or a story that students have read. They are to draw one picture that tells what the chart or story is all about.

165. Vocabulary: Provide a box or envelope containing circles, squares, triangles and other shapes of different sizes and colors. Put slips of paper in the box on which are written, big, bigger, biggest; small, smaller, smallest; wide, wider, widest; dark, darker, darkest; light, lighter, lightest; tall, taller, tallest, etc. Students write the words on their papers, locate appropriate shapes and paste them above the words.

166. Main Idea: Many classroom activities can be made by students as they practice the particular skill. Provide five action pictures. Put possible titles (main idea) for each picture on separate cards. Students match titles to pictures. Then they find five more pictures. Decide on titles and add pictures and titles to the collection.

167. Classification: Think of thirty words representing three different topics. Tell the student the name of the topic (animals, birds, flowers, for example). The student places the words under the appropriate label. Examples:

Animals	Birds	Flowers
pony	robin	rose
rabbit	crow	tulip
woodchuck	sparrow	violet
raccoon	swallow	daisy
squirrel	starling	lily
tiger	cardinal	daffodil
lion	nuthatch	geranium
camel	chickadee	marigold

Other topics could be colors, numbers, furniture, food.

168. Following Directions: Write statements on slips of paper such as: A little red square is to the left of a big blue circle. Students copy a statement on a piece of paper and then paste appropriate shapes above it. To save their time, have the shapes available.

169. Vocabulary: Students with learning disabilities often have difficulty understanding the seasons. Make four posters labeled, Fall, Winter, Spring, and

Summer. They are to locate and paste appropriate pictures and words on the posters.

170. Understanding relationships: Write a series of statements like the following on a card.

_____ is bigger than _____
_____ is smaller than _____
_____ is round
_____ is square
_____ can go faster than _____
_____ is good to eat
_____ can jump over _____
_____ plays with _____
_____ grows in _____
_____ likes to eat _____

Using pictures cut from old spelling, language, reading and math workbooks, students complete the statements. To do the first one, for example, they might choose pictures of a house and a car. They would paste the house on their paper, then write, "is bigger than," and then paste the car on to complete the statement. They can then make up more statements.

171. Vocabulary and Classification: *Who, What, When, Where* and *Why* are difficult words to learn. In addition, some students cannot remember what they mean. Put each of the words on cards. Then make up appropriate words and phrases and put them on cards. Students can sort them according to the words. Some students might have to start with only two words. Appropriate words and phrases could be:

Who	*What*	*When*
an actor	the yellow house	in the afternoon
father	three flowers	one day
the girl	the calendar	in a week
two people	several books	as soon as possible

Jean	some paper	three o'clock
a baseball team	a clock	during the night
a fireman	walked fast	before dark
the President	painted a fence	two years ago
my teacher	rang a bell	after recess
a fourth grader	won the game	at the sound of the bell

Where	Why
on the grass	because it broke
in the house	since he was late
upstairs	in order to play
down in the cellar	because it snowed
at first base	so they would be warm
behind the net	on account of the children
by the river	due to the fact that
over the fence	for the simple reason that
beyond the garden	because it's dark
above the clouds	in order to hear the bell

172. Vocabulary: From time to time, as students read, suggest that they jot down the longest word they see. List them on the board, have them pronounced and discuss their meanings.

173. Classification: Use newspaper grocery ads. Have students list items in specific categories such as meats, vegetables, things that cost less than a dollar, canned food, frozen food, dairy products, etc.

174. Sequence: Have students take turns listening to a cassette recording of a story. After listening, each student draws a picture of a favorite part. When everyone has had a chance the pictures are arranged in correct sequence. A story is dictated or written to go with the pictures and all are stapled together to make a class book.

175. Vocabulary: Work on words that show spatial relationships by creating pictures with cut-outs from

magazines. Example: Paste a picture of a house *in the middle of* a piece of paper. Put a tree *beside* the house. Put some flowers *near* the tree. Put a dog *in front of* the house. Put a bird *on top of* the tree. Put a car *by* the tree.

176. Vocabulary: Provide a box of prepositional phrases such as on the box, under the box, over the box, etc. (above, in, below, behind). Also put pictures of balls (small circles) and pictures of boxes (squares) in the box. Students copy the phrases and illustrate each one by pasting a "ball" in the proper relation to the "box."

177. Sequence: Retype simple stories of five or six sentences putting each sentence on a separate strip. Use different colored paper for each story. Students sequence the stories and copy them.

178. Vocabulary: Students could build word pyramids. Start with a noun. Examples:

flowers	car
tall pretty	new red
yellow pink white	small fast shiny

179. Imagery: Write a sentence on the board that describes something. Students draw a picture to illustrate the sentence. Compare the pictures and discuss the variations. Relate the discussion to the importance of visualizing when reading. Sentences could be:

The little girl was picking flowers.
See the pretty bird in the tree.

180. Vocabulary: Have students make word and picture collages for general terms such as *man* and *woman*.

Paste overlapping pictures on a poster. Write the words on cards and paste them on top of the pictures. Some words for man might be: father, he, him, his, himself, grandfather, son, brother, uncle, nephew, king, duke, sir, Mr., gentleman, husband, men, male, masculine. Let students discover these words for themselves.

181. Vocabulary: Collect color words. Students could take them from their reading and from dictionaries. Look up *red* in a dictionary and you will probably find *scarlet, vermillion,* and *cherry.* Look up *cherry* and you will probably find *cerise.* Other shades of red are *cardinal, pink, ruby,* and *carmine.* The art teacher may be able to supply samples of the various shades of color.

182. Sequence: A popular activity for sequencing is to cut comic strips apart for students to put back together again. Choose those that tell a complete story. Mounting them on different colored paper takes a little longer, but would keep them from getting all mixed up when stored in the same box or envelope. Another way of marking them is to draw a colored border around each strip.

183. Details: Use an interesting action picture from a magazine. Make a list of words, phrases or sentences that pertain and do not pertain to the picture. The student is to choose those that pertain. The student then finds another picture and makes a similar activity.

184. Following directions: Give students specific written directions for drawing a picture. Display all the pictures. Were they all the same? Why or why not? Should they be the same?

185. Vocabulary: To help students understand adjectives, have them draw a series of pictures beginning with the name of a thing or object and then adding more descriptive information. The student should see only one direction at a time. Examples:

a ball
a big red ball
a big red ball with a blue stripe around the middle
a truck
a red truck
a red trailer truck
a red trailer truck with a flat tire

186. Using context: Some people think that much of reading is checking words in context with one's expectations. Students with learning disabilities often have no expectations. They just plod along word by word. To help them develop this skill, provide unfinished phrases or short sentences to be completed. Examples:

table and _____ , boys and _____ , brother and _____ , Jump up and _____ , as fast as you _____ , what time is _____ , where are you _____ , he wagged his _____ , sweep with a _____ , mail the _____ , thank you very _____ .

187. Classification: Have students make classification games. Give them categories such as furniture, clothing; hot, cold; red, yellow; smooth, rough; etc. They locate and cut out pictures and paste them on oaktag cards. Later students sort the cards. (If colored dots are placed on the backs, the cards will be self-checking.)

188. Vocabulary: Make a box of phrases and meanings to be matched. Examples:

as fast as possible - quickly
as soon as - after
throughout the - during
as long as - while
in a leisurely way - slowly
since coming here - continuously
due to the fact - because
except that - but
in addition to - also
even if - although
as a result of - therefore
in defiance of - despite

189. Following directions: Put some light blue paper and a box of crayons in a box. Add directions for making pictures. The students are to draw the pictures using only the crayons. Then they should add directions for other pictures. Example: Draw a brown house with a red roof. Put a tree next to the house. Have one branch sticking out away from the house. Put a blue bird on the branch. Make some red flowers around the tree. Make the rest of the ground green.

190. Details: Collect pictures from newspapers and write two or three sentences describing each. Students are to match descriptions to pictures, then cut out five more pictures, write descriptions and add them to the collection.

191. Vocabulary: Help students become aware of the many different ways we have of expressing ourselves by making lists of words that can be used in place of *said* and *went*. They will find them in the books they read. Some words noted for *said* are: mumbled, called, asked, laughed, giggled, whined, yelled, shrieked, promised, stammered, whispered, replied, shouted, screamed, gasped, inquired, inter-

rupted, snorted, cried, answered, questioned, grumbled, groaned, exclaimed, sighed, crooned, blurted, stuttered.

192. Vocabulary: Some students have difficulty seeing relationships and thinking in abstract terms. They are to cut pictures of any two objects from a magazine, paste them on paper, and write how they are alike in as many different ways as possible. Which comparison was the best (most abstract)? Put a star by it. Example:

Pictures of a shoe and a tie

wear them	manufactured
same color	can buy them
*clothing	for a man

193. Vocabulary and Imagery: To help students appreciate the power of adjectives, have them find a sentence in a story with at least two adjectives and illustrate it. Then have them rewrite the sentence changing the adjectives and illustrate that sentence. Compare the pictures. This is even more effective when done by partners. After illustrating a sentence, the student rewrites it leaving a blank for the adjectives. The partner supplies the adjectives and makes an illustration. Examples:

The *brown* rabbit had *big* ears.
The *white* rabbit had *pink* ears.

The *big red* dog lived in a *green* house.
The *white spotted* dog lived in a *fire*house.

194. Vocabulary: Choose words like big, small, happy, sad, hot, cold, love, hate, and have students cut pictures from magazines to illustrate them. They could make a poster, collage or a mobile.

195. Vocabulary: As students read books have them collect words or sentences that tell whether the story takes place in the present, past, or future.

196. Imagery: Illustrating books is a special art. One thing illustrators have to do is decide what parts of a book to illustrate. Have students choose a favorite book and look at the illustrations. Did the illustrator choose the best parts? Find a part that is not illustrated and make an illustration for it.

197. Imagery: Choose a descriptive poem like *America The Beautiful, Trees,* or a children's poem. Students are to illustrate it using pictures cut from magazines. The poem should appear as a book. The lines that are illustrated should be written along the bottom of each page under the illustration.

198. Main Idea: Cut and mount pictures of books from book ads. On separate strips of oaktag, write a statement for each book that would complete a question like, "In which book would you probably find _____?" Depending on the titles of the books, statements could be:

     a story about a monster
     how to fish
     what causes earthquakes
     where to ski

     Students are to match statements to books.

199. Pronouns: Misunderstanding pronouns causes many comprehension problems. Make up sentences or use sentences from children's stories that have pronouons. Underline the pronouns. Students are to write the pronouns and indicate the words they refer to by writing those words. For example:

Tony had a blue balloon. *It* was on a string.
People were watching *him*. *They* were smiling.
It - balloon
him - Tony
they - people

200. Following directions: Provide a large piece of paper for a picture. This could be placed on a bulletin board or the whole project could become a mural. Put directions for drawing a picture on cards, one direction on each card. Students choose a card and follow the directions. After the picture is completed, read each direction and have students judge whether or not the directions were followed correctly. (If you want, students could put their names on the backs of the cards. Also if you want to add a written activity, have students write what they *did*. For example, if one direction was, "Make a little pumpkin next to the boy," the student would write on the back of the card, "I *made the* little pumpkin next to the boy."

201. Sequence and Main Idea: Using an old chart or story that students have read, make an illustrated book. Draw a light line across drawing paper about two inches from the bottom. The first sentence should be written below the line. A picture illustrating the sentence goes above the line. Each sentence should be placed on a different piece of paper. The cover should have a title (main idea) and a picture. Books can be made by one student or each person in a group can do one page.

202. Punctuation: Print short sentences on strips of paper leaving off punctuation. Make the strips about a half inch longer than the sentences. Provide cards with periods, question marks, and exclamation points. Students read the sentences and put correct

punctuation at end with a paper clip. Examples:
The boy walked down the street
Where is my dog
Watch out

203. Sequence: Cut short stories and news items from children's magazines and weeklies. Cut them apart by paragraphs and mount the paragraphs of each story on different colored paper. Put them in an envelope for students to sequence and read. After they can do this they can add similar activities to the envelope.

204. Following Directions: Have students write directions for others to follow. Exchange papers and try to follow the directions. Discuss the difficulties. Then have students rewrite the directions.

205. Details: To help students note details, have them add an illustration to a book they have read and put in as many details as possible.

206. Vocabulary: Students with perceptual problems are often socially inept. They misjudge social situations and say or do the wrong thing. Have them collect polite phrases from the books they read and try to use them in appropriate situations. Examples:
Thanks, Excuse me, Sorry, Please.

207. Vocabulary: Students could notice words in their books that refer to sounds. Examples: crunch, chime, clang, clatter, wail, sizzle, pop, bang.

208. Vocabulary: Make vocabulary books. Some students might add a word a week while others could add a word a day. The words could come from books they read. They should be illustrated or defined in words that would be meaningful to the student. Don't have

them copy definitions from a dictionary.

209. Vocabulary: Many students with learning disabilities have difficulty with words with multiple meanings. Give them such words and have them write sentences to show the different meanings. Examples:

A bird can *fly*.   I have a *ring* on my finger.
See the *fly* on the screen.   Do you have a key *ring*?

Some common words with more than one meaning are: cry, mouth, left, right, bat, train, rock, block, check, sock, face, bank, roll, saw, tip, pen, box, duck, fast, glass, jar, letter, spring, miss, mean, tie, tire, well, wave, bark.

210. Vocabulary: Make a box of homonyms. Make one card for each pair of homonyms. Students choose cards and write two sentences to illustrate the two meanings. Some homonyms are: red-read, see-sea, so-sew, sent-cent, blue-blew, no-know, meat-meet, wood-would, ant-aunt, mail-male, son-sun, road-rode, by-buy, made-maid, week-weak, right-write, flower-flour, dear-deer, eight-ate, tail-tale, there-their, I-eye, hour-our.

As students find more homonyms they should add them to the box.

211. Following directions: Write diretions for students to follow to make a picture of an object. After they have followed the directions correctly, have them make something and write their own directions. Be sure they make the picture before trying to write the directions. They should sign their names to their directions as revisions might be necessary after another student tries to follow them. Example:

Draw two vertical lines two inches long, parallel to each other, and an inch and a half apart.

Beginning at the top of the left line and ending at the top of the right line, draw a semi-circle that goes above the two lines. Now draw a similar semi-circle that goes below the two lines. (It will look like an oval.)

Make a semi-circle that connects the two lines at the bottom and goes below the lines.

Draw a little circle that will just touch the middle of the left line.

Do you have a picture of a mug?

212. Sequence: After students read books, have them list five or ten main events on cards. Another student reads the book and puts the cards in correct order.

213. Punctuation: Some comprehension problems occur because students ignore or don't understand punctuation. Make typewritten copies of charts or cut paragraphs from old workbooks. Retype them leaving out all punctuation. Laminate them. Two students work together. One reads the punctuated selection while the other puts the punctuation in the unpunctuated copy using a washable marker. After checking, they wipe off the correct punctuation.

214. Details: To help students focus on details, have them read a story and make up questions about it that begin with the following words: Is, Can, Are, Was, Were, Do, Does, Did, Have, Has

215. Sequence: Familiar children's stories like *The Three Bears* and *The Gingerbread Boy* are often pictured in reading workbooks. These and any others with a definite sequence can be cut out, mounted, and given to students to place in sequence.

They can be made self checking by putting a colored dot on the back of each picture, or even on the front, and building an answer sheet. One series might be colored red, yellow, green, blue, orange, and the answer sheet would show this.

216. Vocabulary: Make individual vocabulary boxes for students using their vocabulary books (See above #208) or make a vocabulary box for a group using the daily words (See above #151). Put the words on pink cards and the definitions on blue cards (or use other colors). Students match words to definitions.

217. Vocabulary: One way to increase vocabulary is to focus on synonyms and antonyms. Start a collection on cards for students to match. All the words could be on the same color cards or to make it easier, use one color for synonyms and a different color for antonyms. Synonyms for a beginning reader are: jump-leap, begin-start, happy-glad, angry-mad, answer-reply, truck-van, pretty-beautiful, big-large, hat-cap, car-auto, penny-cent, cup-mug, fast-quick, gift-present, go-leave, gone-left, love-like, house-home, I-me, shop-store, small-little, silent-quiet. Antonyms are: hot-cold, come-go, above-below, add-subtract, after-before, all-none, awake-asleep, good-bad, boy-girl, big-little, begin-end, buy-sell, close-open, early-late, dry-wet, up-down, city-country, yes-no, new-old, push-pull, give-take, stop-go, day-night, empty-full, happy-sad, front-back, small-large, left-right, hard-soft, love-hate, inside-outside, first-last, laugh-cry.

218. Details: Use an advertisement for an elaborate game or toy from a mail order catalogue and make up questions about it that a person should ask before buying it. Examples of types of questions:

What does the item cost?
Is postage extra? If so, how much?
Are batteries needed? If so, how many?
Does the item come assembled?
What age level would probably enjoy the toy or game?

219. Sequence: Use "reaction" sheets that call for the sequence of events. In the book that you have just read, what happened

First _____

Next _____

Then _____

Last _____

or

List three important things that happened in the order in which they happened:

1. _____

2. _____

3. _____

220. Imagery: As students read have them locate sentences in their books that illustrate the five senses. Expect samples like:

Far away on the mountain, he could see two people skiing. (Sight)

He had to shout because of the noisy machines. (Hearing)

The cotton was so soft. (Touch)

One whiff and you knew it was apple pie. (Smell)

Do you want chocolate or vanilla? (Taste)

221. Vocabulary: Make a sufficient number of word cards for *who, what, when, where,* and *why.* Think of sentences that begin with these words and print them on a large piece of oaktag, leaving a blank space for the first word. Make the blank big enough so that a word card will fit. Students are to read the incomplete sentences and complete them with the proper words. Some sentences could have more

than one word. Examples:

_____ is your name	_____ will the plane leave
_____ were you born	_____ do you live
_____ do we have to do it	_____ are they going
_____ is the prettiest	_____ did they do
_____ time is it	_____ paint it blue
_____ not	_____ comes next
_____ is vacation	_____ won
_____ are you wearing	_____ will win the game
_____ kind of cake is it	_____ do you expect her

222. Details: Advertisements for groceries require reading for details. Cut such ads from newspapers, and make up a series of questions to which students could write answers. Examples:

When does this special offer end?
How many coupons are there?
What meat is on sale?
What brand coffee would be the cheapest?

223. Sequence: Discuss words that signal sequence: first, second, third, next, last, then, finally, after, later, before. Put the words on the board or on a chart. As students read they are to note such words and either write or be prepared to indicate a seqence. For example, if the sentence were, "First they had to wash their hands, then they were told to cut up the apples, and finally they could put the apples in the pie," the sequence would be indicated

1. wash hands
2. cut apples
3. put apples in pie

224. Vocabulary: Encourage students to develop a hobby or an interest in a special topic, and collect words related to it. These could be written in a special book. A stamp collector might have a book called, *My Stamp Words* or *My Stamp Dictionary*. Some

words might be: cancellation, cover, philatelist, block, perforation, commemorative, watermark.

225. Vocabulary: Provide the following "reaction" sheet. In the book you have just read:

Who did something? _____

What did they do? _____

When did they do it? _____

Where did they do it? _____

Why did they do it? _____

226. Idioms: Many students with learning disabilities have difficulty with idioms. They tend to take the literal meanings. Have students "collect" idioms. They may hear people using them in conversation and they will read them in stories. You might want to begin with certain types of idioms such as those related to the human body. There are hundreds of these. Some are: all thumbs, green thumb, catch one's breath, see through, over one's head, go to one's head, head over heels, lose one's head, rocks in one's head, head in the clouds, off the top of one's head, head and shoulders above, hair stood on end, on one's toes, underfoot, cold feet, shake a leg, stand up for, stand on one's own two feet, kick up one's heels, take to one's heels, lend a hand, handful, wash one's hands of, on one's hands, up in arms, hands down, keep an eye on, set eyes on, catch one's eye, pull the wool over one's eyes, keep one's word, pick one's brain, all ears, keep an ear to the ground.

227. Vocabulary: Have a root for a week. Everyone looks for words made from the root. If the root were *aqua*, meaning water, some words would be: aquarium, aqualung, aquaduct, aquaplane.

228. Vocabulary: Take a common word and have students list synonyms that would make the word more specific or more interesting. After a few words are listed, some students could look them up in a dictionary. The definitions will suggest more and more synonyms. Example: *seat,* chair, armchair, love seat, couch, sofa, divan, rocker, bench, stool, cricket, hassock, lounger, settee, settle, beach chair, captain's chair, straight chair, side chair, high chair, wheel chair, Morris chair.

229. Vocabulary: Make horizontal word puzzles. Write a story or a factual statement. Put the words on a grid beginning at the top left hand square. Make a black square after each word. Put numbers starting with one by the first letter of each word. Make a copy of the puzzle leaving the numbers in, but leaving out the words. Then put the numbers in a column under the puzzle and write a clue for each word. For example, if the first four words in the puzzle were, "One day a boy," the clues could be:

1. A number
2. Rhymes with hay
3. First letter of alphabet
4. Will be a man

230. Fact and Opinion: Cut out magazine ads for food, clothing, jewelry, sports equipment, or some other item. The student finds five facts and five opinions.

231. Inference: After reading each chapter of a book, students make out a card to answer one of the following sets of questions:

Tell one thing that happened.
Why did it happen?

Tell one thing that somebody did.
Why did they do it?

232. Inference: To help students understand inferences, have them provide information that is not stated in a story. Choose such sentences and encourage elaboration. Example:

Ten-year-old James was just about to go out when his mother called, "James! I want to see you before you go out." He could tell from her voice that he was in trouble again.

What are some things James might have done to get into trouble?

Mr. Jones came out of the grocery store carrying a very big bag.

What do you suppose was in the bag?

233. Details: Students can improve their ability to note details. Show them a tiny object and have them write a description of it. Then have them draw a greatly enlarged picture of the object and write another description. Compare the two descriptions.

234. Imagery: Use an interesting action picture. Have students list what they see. Then list what they "hear."

235. Sequence: Using an action picture, have students write what happened just before the picture and just after the picture. If these were written on cards, they could be kept in an envelope with the picture and students who have difficulty doing the activity could choose appropriate before and after cards to reconstruct the story.

236. Imagery: Display an action picture. Have descriptions written focusing on sight. Then have them rewritten focusing on sound or some other sense.

237. Imagery: Have students choose illustrations from books they are reading, and answer the question, "In what ways did the illustrations *add* to the story?"

238. Imagery: Give students "scenes" to complete by writing more information. Each "scene" would be a sentence. The student would be expected to add more details to the "picture." The "scenes" could be taken from books or just made up. The sentence, "Mary was sitting on her front porch," tells very little, for example. What was Mary sitting on? How old was Mary? What does she look like? How is she dressed? What kind of house does she have? What color is it? etc. Students should write a full description. The original sentence would not have to be used.

239. Inference: Use a picture with lots of action. Tell students that they are in the picture and have them write what they are doing.

240. Imagery: As students read books suggest that they locate sentences that specifically tell about the illustrations, and sentences that give other information. For example, a sentence from a story might be, "A funny little green man from outer space landed in the garden." There could be a picture of the man in the garden. The next sentence might be, "In no time, the man sprang up to my shoulder and began to shout in my ear." There might not be a picture for this.

241. Identifying facts: Some facts are more important than others, but students don't always realize this. As they read they can find one important fact and one unimportant fact. Using a social studies assignment, have them list five important facts and star the most important one.

242. Summaries: Very often the important points of a newspaper story are summarized in the caption under a picture. Cut out suitable pictures and have students write captions. They will not be the same

as the newspaper captions, but they should be plausible. The actual captions could be pasted to the backs of the pictures to be compared with the students' captions just for fun. Examples of captions:

A sudden wind storm broke many branches and uprooted trees in the north end of town.

The swim team had its final practice today before the championship meet. Last year they came in third and they hope to better that tomorrow.

243. Fact and Opinion: Prepare statements of fact and opinion. After classifying them, students add ten more. These could provide an additional learning experience if they were related to a specific subject.

Examples: Mark Fact or Opinion

The score was five to two.   Fact
The visiting team was terrible.   Opinion
Yesterday was quite hot.   Opinion
The clock is not working.   Fact
He has a new car.   Fact
He bought the best car.   Opinion.

244. Inference: Assign the students a paragraph in a social studies book to read or provide an informational paragraph. They are to make up questions for each sentence. If one of the sentences were, "Alaska is the largest state in the Union," some questions might be, What is the smallest state? How big is Alaska? How much of Alaska is livable? How many people live in Alaska? How does that compare with the other states? Isn't there something more important to say about Alaska? Has Alaska always been the largest state? What is the next largest state?

245. Tests: Students with severe reading problems are often fearful of written tests. Everyone has to learn

to take tests alone, but one can learn in a group first. Make a group responsible for answering test questions. Each person in the group is equally responsible and everyone gets the same mark.

246. Facts: Using a factual account or a social studies book, have students write five questions that can be answered from reading the selection and five questions about the same topic that cannot be answered.

247. Categories: Give students the following list of words: cat, dog, mouse, rabbit. Tell them to think of a word that tells about all the others and write it above the words. (Animals) Give them more lists to categorize. Examples:
Boston, New York, Atlanta, Portland (Cities)
Atlantic, Pacific, Arctic, Indian (Oceans)
Summer, Winter, Fall, Spring (Season)
North America, South America, Africa, Asia, Europe
(Continents)
When they can do this tell them to use words from a social studies book and make up five more lists.

248. Questions: Show students how to decide on questions to ask themselves as they read their texts. Have them take a chapter from a social studies book and rewrite every sub-head as a question. Later they can answer their questions.

249. Summaries: Let students choose any two paragraphs from the books they are reading and summarize each paragraph in one sentence.

250. Summaries: An effective way to help students summarize is to have them rewrite stories for younger children. After choosing an appropriate story, they take it chapter by chapter and list two or three important events for each chapter. Then they read their lists to see if the story makes sense and also to see if anything can be omitted. The story can then be written and illustrated.

PART IV
BOOK SHARING
PROJECTS

BOOK SHARING PROJECTS

Sharing reading with others is a vital part of a reading program. Thinking about the story to decide what type of project to do, and then choosing something that would be unique to the story, fosters critical thinking. Sharing projects with classmates not only gives satisfaction to the one who does the project, but also motivates others to read. Thus, projects should not be thought of as rewards for the few. Everyone should have opportunities to share books through projects.

There are three types of book projects: oral, written, and arts and crafts. Oral projects range from choosing and reading a favorite part aloud to acting out the story or presenting it as a puppet or marionette show. Books can be read aloud to younger children or discussed with peers. They can be presented as book talks or recorded with sound effects and musical background. Oral presentations seem easy, but they are not. They require considerable organization and depend on audience acceptance.

Written projects are the more traditional approach, but the projects themselves need not be the traditional book report. If the book is about people and pets, the story can be rewritten from the point of view of the pet, an incident from a book can be rewritten as a newspaper article, another chapter can be added or a different ending proposed. Parts of the book can be told in the form of a diary kept by one of the characters. The book can be discussed in an imaginary letter to a friend, or a letter can be written to the author. Written projects are the most difficult, but should be the ultimate goal. A literate person reads and writes. Students with severe reading disabilities, though, would be incapable of doing written projects. The best type for them are the arts and crafts projects.

Arts and crafts projects also require organization and thinking, but they do not require the presenter to come face to face with an audience and, of course, they don't require writing ability. They can be displayed in hallways, classrooms, and libraries to be admired by everyone. It isn't even necessary to have the student's name on the project. Students with severe reading disabilities are often good artists. Making such projects helps them feel better about themselves. Many times it is possible to have those with reading disabilities teach their classmates how to make the projects.

The fifty projects in this section (Activities 251-300) require very little writing beyond the name of a book and author. This does not preclude writing. Those who can write should be encouraged to add descriptive material and scripts for puppets.

Although intended as book projects, all fifty can be used as "experiences" with beginning readers in a language experience approach. The first one, for example, could be a student's favorite book or comic character. While making it the student would be encouraged to talk about the character. Then a story would be dictated. The advantage of this is that the dictated story would be at the maturity level of the student.

You will notice that the directions for the projects are written to the student. Since they are for students with severe reading disabilities, it is not intended that students be able to read the directions. They should be read and explained to them. The projects are listed in approximate order of difficulty, the first one requiring very little time and no writing. It is hoped that these projects will be used to help students see that reading is enjoyable.

251. **PAPER STAND-UP CHARACTER**

Fold a little square of paper in half. Then open it out and stand it up. This is how your book character will stand. Now put it flat on your desk or table and draw the character on the square, and cut it out leaving the bottom part so it will be able to stand.

252. **SEE INSIDE THE HOUSE**

Make an outline drawing of the front of the house in your book. Put in the door and windows. Cut out the house. Then carefully cut around three sides of the door and the windows so that they will fold open. Put paste around the edges of the house and paste it to a piece of manila drawing paper leaving a space at the bottom for the name of the book and the author. Behind the door and windows draw people, animals, or things related to your book.

253. **BOOK MOBILE**

Cut a strip of oaktag about two inches wide and sixteen inches long. Punch six holes in it. (See diagram on next page.) Put the name of the book and author on the strip, and then staple the short ends together. Tie a piece of yarn or string about ten inches long in each of the top three holes, and knot them together. This will be used to hang the mobile. Decide on three things that are important in the book and make little pictures of them. Cut out the pictures. Punch holes in the tops of the pictures and tie them to the oaktag strip.

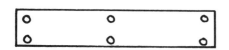

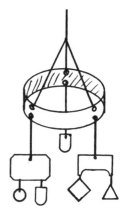

254. BUMPER STICKER

Make a bumper sticker to get people to read your book. You could begin by using the title of the book, but then try to think of another line that would make people think, laugh, or feel good about themselves.

255. OAKTAG "DOLL" CHARACTERS

Make your main character out of oaktag parts — body, head, arms and legs, and attach them together with brass paper fasteners. Find some scrap material and make clothes for your character. Use yarn for hair.

256. SHOE BOX SCENE

Choose a scene from a book and make a three dimensional picture of it in a shoe box. First decorate the inside of the box by painting it or by pasting paper on it. If it's a room scene, the sides of the box would be the walls. You can find pictures of clocks, bookcases, lamps, etc. to paste on the walls. Then make furniture out of paper, little boxes, spools, and other scrap material. People can be made of oaktag and dressed in scraps of material. If you make an outdoor scene, you can have airplanes and birds flying by hanging them with thread. Be sure to put the name of the book and author on the top of the box.

257. TISSUE PAPER ANIMALS

If your book is about animals, make some large tissue paper models. First make an outline drawing of one of the animals. Put the tissue paper over the outline and trace it. Do this twice because you need two copies. Cut them out. Save the scraps. Use crayons to add eyes and any other necessary features or clothing. Then put glue around the edge of one, *except along the back*, and glue the two pieces together. After the glue is dry, stuff more tissue paper through the hole you left in the back. When the animal is nice and plump, glue the hole to close it. Hang the animals from the ceiling.

258. ORIGAMI CHARACTERS

Use origami, the Japanese art of paper folding, to show the characters of your book. For directions get a book on origami from the library. Two easy characters to begin with are a cat and a dog. Use a piece of paper that is about four to six inches square. The paper must be a perfect square. In the diagrams, the dotted lines indicate a fold.

1.
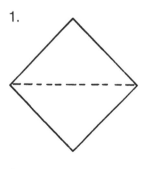

2.
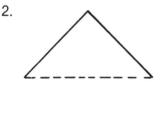

3.

4.
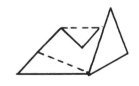

continued

5.

Turn this over.

6.

Glue circles on for eyes.

To make a dog, follow the first three diagrams. Then turn the paper over so that the shortest side is on the bottom. Fold the points down to make ears.

4.

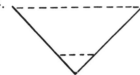

5.

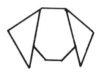

259. DECORATED CUBE

Make a cube out of paper. Before gluing it together, put the title and author of the book on one side, and decorate the other sides with scenes from the book. Example of a pattern for a cube:

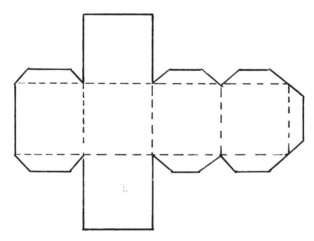

260. UNDERWATER SCENE

If your book has an underwater scene, you can make it in a shoe box. Color the inside of the box blue. Use crumpled green and blue paper for water. Hang fish on threads so they will move. When the scene is complete, cover the opening of the box with blue plastic. Put the name of the book and the author on the top of the box.

261. SHALLOW DIORAMA

Show an outdoor scene from your book in a box lid. Make a picture on the inside of the lid for the background scene. Then add objects to complete the scene. Use twigs, bark, grasses, wild flowers, leaves, and pebbles. Put the name of the book and the author on a little square of oaktag and hang it from a sign post in the corner.

262. POSTER

Make a poster to "sell" your book. Draw a picture of a character or scene from the book and make up a saying to put on the poster like, YOU WILL L♡VE THIS BOOK.

263. COLLAGE

Look through magazines to find pictures that could illustrate your book. If the book were CHARLOTTE'S WEB by E. B. White, for example, you could find pictures of a spider, flies, pig, rat, lamb, goose, horses, cocker spaniel, barn, county fair, farm scene, a girl, an ax, a nursing bottle, pail, farmer, fence, and cars that brought people to see the web. One section could show the various things that Wilbur ate (pancakes, a third of a gingersnap, toast, orange peel, etc.). Add important words like Some Pig, Terrific, Radiant, Humble, Zuckerman's Famous Pig, and the names of the people and animals in the story. Tear around the pictures and paste them so that they overlap. Be sure to indicate the name of the book and the author.

264. MAKE OR SHOW SOMETHING

In many books, one of the characters cooks or makes something very special or does something unusual. Maybe one of the characters made an apple pie or did a magic trick. When you read a book in which a character did something special you do it, too, and bring it to school to show everyone.

265. FLANNEL BOARD STORY

Turn a small gift box into a flannel board story of your book. Glue a piece of flannel to the inside of the lid. Then cut out of paper whatever characters and things are necessary to tell part or all of the story. Make them small enough to fit on the lid when you tell the story. Glue a small square of flannel on the back of the pictures so they will stick to the flannel on the lid. Store them all in the box. Put the name of the book and the author on the outside of the box.

266. BOOK CHARACTER SITTING

Collect as many old spools as you have characters. Make the characters out of paper. First you have to get the right size for the spool. For most, cut a rectangular piece of paper about as wide as a spool and 4½ inches long. Think of it as a tall person and bend it to sit on the spool. When you are satisfied with the size, cut some out of oaktag. If you want, you can decide where the arms should be and cut them, too, or you can add the arms later. Make and color your book characters and have them sit together on spools. Put a card with them indicating the name and author of the book.

267. MINIATURE STAGE SET

Choose an important scene from your book and make it into a miniature stage set. Use a shoe box for the stage. Put a string across the top of the opening for the curtain. Then paint the background scene and place necessary props and people made out of paper and scraps.

268. SCARF

Cut a piece of an old sheet into a square or a rectangle large enough for a scarf. An old colored sheet would be especially pretty. Hem it. Make a decorative border around the edge and fill up the inside with pictures and words related to your book. Color everything with marking pens that have permanent ink.

269. BOOKMARK

Make a special bookmark. Put the name of your book and author on one side and a scene from the book on the other. To make the bookmark:

1. Cut a strip of oaktag six by one and a half inches.

2. Punch a hole in the center of one end.

3. Take a piece of yarn about eight inches long and fold it in half. Put the loop through the hole, and draw the loose ends through the loop.

4. After putting the design on, you can cover it with clear contact paper.

270. BALL CHARACTER

Poke a hole in an old ball just large enough for your middle finger to fit in it. This will be the head. Decorate it to look like a character in your book. Then take a piece of cloth about the size of a handkerchief and put it over your middle finger. Put your finger in the hole in the ball. Gather some cloth around your thumb and some around your little finger and secure with rubber bands. Your fingers become your character's arms. Now that you can see how it will work, take it apart and decorate it to look like a character in your book.

271. FLAT MOBILE

Cut a strip of oaktag long enough to print the name of the book and author on it. Attach pictures and words related to the book. The pictures should be cut out to show their shapes and the words should be on different shaped cards if appropriate. The word *snow,* on a snow shape, for example. If you want, you could label some pictures by hanging them from little strips of oaktag. You could do this for the main characters, for example. Tack the "mobile" to a bulletin board.

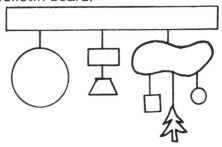

272. PAPER BAG CHARACTER

Use a small paper bag to make a puppet of the main character of your book. The bottom fold will be the mouth. Put your hand in the bag and move it to open and close the fold to see how it works. Then add eyes, nose, mouth and hair in appropriate places. You can put the name of the character, the book and author on the back of the bag.

273. TANGRAM FIGURES

The tangram originated in China. It is a puzzle with only seven simple pieces. They can be combined to make hundreds of recognizable shapes of people, animals, objects, letters, and numbers. The shapes look like silhouettes and the difficult part is to always keep the total shape "solid." You could use a tangram to illustrate something from your book. Get a book of tangrams from the library. The seven tangram pieces and two suggestions follow:

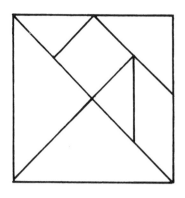 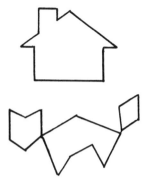

274. MEMORABILIA

Many books have one important item that is necessary to the story. Make a "collection" of these. Examples: Paddington's tag, the piece of jigsaw that was swallowed by Curious George, Harold's purple crayon, Mateo's clay horse, Jennie's hat, the "carrot seed," Rosie's library card, and many, many more.

275. UNIQUE PROJECTS

Think of projects that would be unique to specific books. These would be projects that would not fit any other book. For example, draw a picture of a fence on a long piece of shelf paper and then put Mrs. Ames' twenty seven cats on the fence. Make Midge's basket of turtles, or make a display of Mr. Pine's signs. Make Mr. Popper's penguins, Billy's banjo, the 500th hat of Bartholomew Cubbins, or a great big papier-mâché Clifford.

276. PORTRAIT

Paint a large portrait of a favorite book character. You could find a picture of the character in the book and enlarge it. When you finish, make a frame for it out of oaktag. Put the character's name in the middle of the bottom edge of the frame.

277. PICTURE ALBUM

If your book is about a family, a team, or some other group, or if the main character in the book meets a lot of interesting people, make a picture album. One way to do this is to put three pieces of construction paper on top of each other, and carefully fold them to make a booklet. Poke two holes in the folds, insert yarn, and tie a bow on the outside of the booklet. Draw pictures of the people on the inside pages and write something about each one. If you want it to look like a real picture album, draw the pictures on separate pieces of paper and stick them in the album. Be sure to write something under each picture to explain it. On the outside cover write, "Picture Album" and the name and author of the book.

278. PAPER FINGER PUPPETS

Choose two book characters who say something important to each other and make finger puppets of them out of paper. Your fingers will become their legs! Use oaktag paper and follow the basic shape below. You will have to make the holes just right for the size of your fingers.

279. PAPER BAG HOUSE

If a house is important in your book, make a model of it out of a small paper bag. Stuff the bag with scrap paper until you get your house tall enough, then shut the bag to form the roof. Cut off any extra paper and glue the bag to close it. Paint your house. You can write the name of the book and author on a card and paste it to the bottom of the house.

280. LOLLIPOP CHARACTERS

A whole set of characters and objects can be made on lollipop or other sticks. If you want to make tiny figures, use toothpicks. Make your characters on paper and paint them or use bright marking pens. Then glue them to the sticks. Try using corrugated paper for a different effect. You'll find it in cardboard cartons and in candy boxes.

281. SLOTTED ANIMALS

The animals in your book can be made to stand. For a two-dimensional animal, make a front view of the body and side views of the feet. You will make slots in both and fit them together.

front view   side view of foot (make two)

A three-dimensional animal requires a side view of the body and front views of the legs.

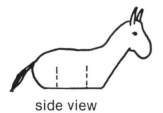

side view   front view (make two)

282. HAND PUPPET CHARACTER

Hand puppet characters can be made out of paper which is glued around the edges or they can be made out of old sheets or other material and stitched together. Put your hand flat on the paper or cloth. Put your three middle fingers together and open out your thumb and little finger as far as you can. They will be the arms of the puppet. Now draw around your hand and your wrist. Look at what you drew. You might want to change the shape of the head. When you are satisfied, use it as a pattern and make two shapes exactly alike. Decorate them and then glue or sew them together. Put it on your hand and make it move.

283. STONE CHARACTERS

A whole book scene can be made of stones. You will have to look for just the right shapes and sizes. When you find them, wash them, and then decide what characters you will make. You can glue stones together with Elmer's Glue and you can paint them with tempera or poster paint. You can also glue on buttons, pieces of felt, and other things. When you no longer want the book project, you can use the decorated stones for paperweights that will continue to remind you of the book. Glue a piece of felt on the bottom to protect your desk.

284. BIG BOOK DISPLAY

When you read a book that you think is great and you want everyone to know about it, make a big book display out of cardboard cartons. Get three or four grocery cartons each a little smaller than the next. You are going to put them on top of each other. Decide what characters or scenes from your book you want to show. If you have three boxes, you will have twelve sides for display. You could put the name of the book and author on one of them. Cover the sides with colored paper and decorate with characters and scenes from the book, or paint everything on with tempera or poster paint. You could display the book on the top if you like.

285. CONE CHARACTERS

Make a circle. A twelve-inch radius is a good size, but you might like to make smaller characters. Cut the circle in half. Each half can be formed into a cone that will stand. Put the semicircle on your desk or table with the curved side down and sketch your character. It can be a person or an animal. Cut features and clothes from scrap paper and material and paste in appropriate places. Then fold into a cone and staple.

286. GLOVE FINGER PUPPETS

Your book story can be told with finger puppets made on an old glove. Decide on up to five characters. If you want more than five characters, you will need two gloves. Put one glove on your hand and hold your hand so that your palm faces in. Close your hand into a fist. Now put up one finger. That is one character. Notice that you will be making the characters on the backs of the glove fingers so that they will face your audience when you lift your fingers. You will have to decide how you want to make the thumb character or if you want to use your thumb at all. When you are sure how this will work, decorate the glove fingers to look like your book characters.

287. ROLLER MOVIE

Make a list of the most important events in your book and decide which ones will be used so you will know how long your "film" will have to be. Decide if you want the movie to be rolled up and down or sideways. If up and down, make four holes in the sides of an open cardboard carton near the opening and as close to the top and bottom as possible. Put one stick through the two holes at the top, and one stick through the holes at the bottom. These will be the rollers. Old broom handles make good rollers. Measure the distance between the rollers and use this measurement to mark shelf paper into sections. Each section will be a picture. Draw pictures in each section to show the sequence of events in the story. The first section should show the name of the book and the author. Be sure to leave some blank paper at the beginning and end to be attached to the rollers. After the pictures have been completed, tack or tape the ends to the rollers. As you roll the "movie" you can tell about the story.

288. MINIATURE ROLLER MOVIE

Make two cuts in a plastic lid three inches long and 2½ inches apart. Cut a strip of paper a little less than three inches wide and forty inches long. Draw lines across the strip of paper 2½ inches apart. You will have sixteen sections. Leave the first two sections blank, put the name of the book and author on the third section, and "THE END" on the third section from the end. Leave the last two sections blank. There will be ten sections left in the middle. Decide on ten events of the book and draw pictures to illustrate them. Insert the strip through the cuts in the plastic lid and pull to show the movie. Store the movies in the container.

289. WORD PICTURE

Decide on an important person, animal, or thing in your book and plan a word picture. Make a list of words that describe or tell about the person, animal, or thing you chose. Then draw a very light picture of it in pencil. Write the words along the pencil lines to outline your picture. You can use different colors.

290. ABC BOOK

Write the letters of the alphabet in a column. After each leter put the name of a person or thing that begins with that letter and was important to your book. Then staple enough paper together to make a book with twenty-eight pages, one page for the front cover, one for the back cover, and twenty-six for the letters. On the cover print, "AN ABC BOOK ABOUT (name of book) BY (author). Print one letter of the alphabet on each page. Then beginning with A, write the words you chose and an illustration for each.

291. BOOK CHAIN

Make a book chain for a story that has a definite sequence of events. First make a list of all the events and number them in order. Then write each event on a strip of paper about eight inches long and a half an inch wide. Loop each strip so that the writing is on the outside and link them together to form a chain. You could add a loop in the beginning for the name of the book and author, and a loop at the end for your name.

292. MAKE A BOOK

The ideas in some books can be used to make similar books. For example, after reading HAROLD AND THE PURPLE CRAYON, choose your favorite color and make a book using your name. You can do the same with BRAVE DANIEL, a CLIFFORD BOOK, and many others. GHOSTS AND CROWS AND THINGS WITH O'S invites you to make a book. To make the book itself use three pieces of white paper and one piece of colored for the cover. If possible, have the colored piece just a little larger than the white. Stack them with the colored paper on the bottom and fold them evenly to look like a book. Open carefully and make three holes in the crease with a needle. Put one hole in the middle and the other two about half way between the middle hole and the top or bottom of the book. Sew the pages together with strong thread, embroidery thread, or yarn. Put the needle through the middle hole from the *inside* of the book, and pull the thread through leaving at least three inches to be used later to tie a knot or a bow. Come back through the top hole. Go through the bottom hole from the inside and come back through the middle hole. Tie a knot or a bow.

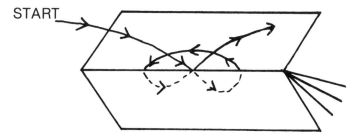

293. MAIN CHARACTER POSTER

Make an outline drawing of a main character or just the character's head. Make it in the middle of a large sheet of paper so that there is plenty of room all around it. Then add pictures and words that would describe the characer, tell what the character is like, tell about the character's favorite foods, sports, or whatever other information you can get about the character from the book. You might make a line from the character's mouth, for example, leading to some favorite expressions.

294. BANNER

Make a banner on a wire coat hanger to advertise your book. Make it as wide as the hanger and about twice as long. Use construction paper in a color that you think would be appropriate for your book. Put the title, author, and a picture or two on the banner with crayon, markers, or paint. Cut a fringe on the bottom. You can hang the banner from the bottom of the hanger or better you can cover the whole hanger by folding over the top edges. If you do that, you will be able to put a picture in the triangle.

295. DOG SHOW

After you and your friends have read several books about dogs, plan to have a dog show. Use the cardboard from boxes. Make an outline picture of your dog and cut it out. Then paint it with tempera or poster paint. Line up all the dogs to be judged.

296. SCRAPBOOK

As you read your book jot down pictures and things you could collect or make for a scrapbook. Then look through magazines for the pictures and collect or make the things. They might be pictures of houses, people, animals, cars, flashlights, and things like a torn envelope, foreign stamp, bus ticket, etc. depending, of course, on your story. On the outside of the scrapbook put SCRAPBOOK OF and then the name of the book and author. Be sure to write something under each thing you put in the scrapbook to show how it relates to the story.

297. BOOK SCENE

If you have read a book with descriptions of particularly beautiful scenery, make a picture of one of the scenes with pastel chalk on black or dark blue paper. Plan the picture before using the chalk.

298. BOOK JACKET

Design a jacket for your book. Put the name of the book and author and a colorful picture on the front. On the back, put an exciting conversation or a beautiful description from the book. Choose something that you think would make people want to read the book.

299. COMIC STRIP

Take an amusing incident from your book and turn it into a comic strip. If you like doing comic strips, try rewriting the whole story into a comic book.

300. POSTAGE STAMPS

If your book is about American History, start collecting used postage stamps that have pictures of the people or incidents in the story. When you display them, write a note under each one telling how it is related to the book.

PART V
SERVICE WORDS
CHECK LIST OF SKILLS
A NOTE ON THE IEP

SERVICE WORDS

SERVICE WORDS

Reference has been made in the activities to "service" words. These are sometimes called "function" or "sight" words. They are words like *said, was, at, an, had,* and *of.* They have little or no concrete meanings, but are necessary to express ideas and to define concepts. It is almost impossible to say or write a sentence without a "service" word. There are many lists of these words available. The most familiar and widely used is the Dolch Word List. Some others, also known by the names of their authors are, Dale, Harris-Jacobson, Hillerich, Kucera-Francis, and Spache. The lists are not identical although some words are common to all.

If you do not have access to any of the above word lists, the following may be used. It is based on the reading ability of hundreds of first graders taught by many different teachers over a five year period using a language experience approach. These 325 words appeared in the charts they dictated and in the stories they wrote. Some appeared with greater frequency than others so were learned more easily. They have been labeled here as Pre-Primer words and there are seventy five of them. The next hundred words are labeled Primer (1-1). Students who know these one hundred seventy five words would be capable of reading a beginning first grade book. The next hundred and fifty words are labeled First Reader (1-2). Students who know these additional hundred and fifty words would be ready to read a second grade level book.

They would also be expected to be able to read similar words formed by changing the initial consonant or initial blend. For example, the words *fast* and *last* are on the list, so students would be expected to be able to read words like *past* and *blast*.

PRE-PRIMER WORDS:
a an and away
ball big blue but
can car come
dog down
father for fun funny
gave get go good
had has have help her here him hot house
I in is it
jump
keep
let little look
made make man me mother my
no not
oh one
play
red ride run
said see sit six something
ten that the this to toy two
up us
want we went what where will with
you

PRIMER 1-1
after all am any are around ask at
baby barn bed bird birthday black boat box boy
cake came cat children color cow cry cut

day did do doll duck
easy eat
family farm find fish five four
game girl
happy hat he hear hello hill home hop
into
kitten know
land like looked
Miss moon more morning Mr. Mrs.
new now
on our out
penny pie please pony put
quack
ran
saw she small so soon stop street surprise
take thank then there they thing three time too train
under
very
was wanted well who white
yellow yes your

FIRST READER 1-2
about again almost along also animal another as
asked ate
back bark be bear before began behind being book
bring brown bus by
call called can't catch cold corn could country
dance didn't does don't door
egg every
far fast feet felt few first flower food friend from
give glass going good-by got gray green grow
guess
hand head hen hide his hold horse how

if I'm it's
just
large last laugh left line long lost lunch
many may maybe men met mitten must
name need never next night number near
of old once open or other over
paint party pet pocket prize push
rabbit rain read road room
sang sat say school set show side sing sleep slow
snow some sometimes spring stay step stick
stopped story sun
tell than their them these think those today told
tree truck
wagon walk way wet when which wish without
work would

CHECK LIST OF SKILLS

CHECK LIST OF SKILLS

WORD ANALYSIS

As students progress in learning how to read, they acquire phonetic and structural analysis skills that enable them to become independent readers. Most of these skills are mastered by the end of third grade. Skills at higher reading levels are more complex than those at lower levels. Thus, they can be listed in sequential order. It is important for teachers and tutors to be aware of this order so that they will know which skills are appropriate to teach. This is not to say that every student will follow the exact sequence, but it would not be appropriate, for example, to expect a student at a first reader level to identify prefixes and suffixes or to apply phonics to pronounce syllables correctly.

WORD ANALYSIS — First Reader Level

____ 1. Acquires a sight vocabulary (one word a day).
____ 2. States rhyming words.
____ 3. Names letters, both upper and lower case.
____ 4. Writes independently initial consonant of any word beginning with the following fifteen consonants: *b, c, d, f, g, h, j, k, l, m, n, p, r, s, t,* disregarding the different sounds of *c, g,* and *s.*

_____ 5. Writes consonant letters representing sounds at ends of words.

_____ 6. Writes blends in response to a word given orally that begins with any of the following blends: *bl, cl, fl, gl, pl, sl, sc, sk, sm, sn, sp, st, sw, br, cr, dr, fr, gr, pr, tr.*

_____ 7. Recognizes silent consonant letters in *kn* and *wr.*

_____ 8. Pronounces compound words made up of known "service" words.

_____ 9. Recognizes plurals formed by adding *s.*

_____ 10. Pronounces known words when *ing* is added without changing the base form of the word.

_____ 11. Uses context clues and initial consonants to pronounce unknown words.

_____ 12. Uses rhyming elements, known words and common phonograms, to read and write unknown words by substituting consonants in initial position.

_____ 13. States short vowel sounds in one-syllable words when pronounced by a teacher.

_____ 14. Reads all three letter words in CVC pattern.

_____ 15. States number of syllables in a word pronounced by a teacher.

WORD ANALYSIS — Second Reader Level

_____ 1. Reads and writes unknown words ending in phonograms by substituting blends in the initial position.

_____ 2. Writes final blends independently *(ft, nt, rt, rd, rk,* and *st.)*

_____ 3. States long vowel sounds in one-syllable words when pronounced by a teacher.

_____ 4. Reads all words in the CVCe pattern.

_____ 5. Reads and states meanings of contractions

such as: *I'm, I'll isn't, didn't, don't, it's, she's, he's, what's, and can't.*

___ 6. Reads initial consonant digraphs *ch, sh, th, wh.*

___ 7. Reads final consonant digraphs *ck, ch, sh, ng, nk, th.*

___ 8. Reads words containing *er, ir, ur.*

___ 9. Reads words where the root word is changed when *ing, ed, er, est* are added.

___ 10. *Reads words containing diphthongs ou, ow* (as in cow), *oi,* and *oy.*

___ 11. Reads words containing vowel digraphs *ai, ay, ea, ie, oa, oo, ow* (as in blow).

___ 12. Identifies unknown words by using context clues.

___ 13. Reads words where *y* is changed to *i* before *es, er, est,* and *ed.*

___ 14. Determines the number of syllables in an unknown word by the number of possible vowel sounds it contains.

___ 15. Uses a variety of appropriate clues to decode words: picture, rhyming, context, phonetic analysis, and structural analysis.

WORD ANALYSIS — Third Reader Level

___ 1. Pronounces words beginning with three-letter blends: *spr, str, scr, shr, thr, spl, squ.*

___ 2. Pronounces words containing diphthongs *au* and *aw.*

___ 3. Pronounces words containing different sounds of *oo.*

___ 4. Applies four vowel principles CVC, CV, CVVC, and CVCe when reading words.

___ 5. Recognizes exceptions to above principles.

___ 6. Reads and states meanings of contractions such as: we'll, she'll, they'll, you'll, won't, we're, you're, couldn't, I've, she'd, he'd.

_____ 7. Pronounces three different sounds of *ed* at ends of words.

_____ 8. Reads and writes words where consonants are doubled when adding *ing, y, er,* and *est.*

_____ 9. Applies knowledge of phonics to pronounce *c* and *g.*

_____ 10. Reads words containing *ild, ind, old.*

_____ 11. Recognizes and pronounces different sounds of *s.*

_____ 12. Identifies and states meanings of simple prefixes such as *re* and *un.*

_____ 13. Identifies and states meanings of simple suffixes such as *ful* and *less.*

_____ 14. Divides two syllable words by visual inspection, i.e. between two consonants, after single vowel, and before consonant followed by *le.*

_____ 15. Applies phonics to pronounce syllables.

COMPREHENSION

Comprehension abilities are not reflected in a series of skills. Comprehension, because it is related to thinking ability, vocabulary, and background of experience, increases in complexity rather than type. Inferential thinking, for example, takes place at all grade levels. Questions and answers should demand progressively more sophisticated thinking. Being able to answer inferential questions at first reader level does not guarantee similar success at third reader level. Therefore, a check list for *Comprehension* will have some items that are the same at every level. They need to be retaught and rechecked at each level.

COMPREHENSION — First Reader Level

_____ 1. Tells a sensible story about an action picture.

_____ 2. Makes meaningful contributions to charts.

____ 3. Suggests suitable titles for charts.
____ 4. Uses punctuation correctly at ends of sentences.
____ 5. Arranges sentences in correct sequences.
____ 6. Describes likenesses and differences.
____ 7. Answers factual questions.
____ 8. Answers inferential questions.
____ 9. Locates answers to specific questions.
____ 10. Follows writtten directions.

COMPREHENSION — Second Reader Level

____ 1. Classifies and categorizes words.
____ 2. Retells stories in own words.
____ 3. Relates pertinent details.
____ 4. Predicts outcomes of stories.
____ 5. Suggests appropriate titles for stories.
____ 6. Recalls sequence of events.
____ 7. Answers factual questions.
____ 8. Answers inferential questions.
____ 9. Locates answers to specific questions.
____ 10. States main idea.

COMPREHENSION — Third Reader Level

____ 1. Recalls sequence of events.
____ 2. Answers factual questions.
____ 3. Answers inferential questions.
____ 4. Locates answers to specific questions.
____ 5. States main idea.
____ 6. Distinguishes important from unimportant facts.
____ 7. Distinguishes fact from opinion.
____ 8. Infers main idea.

____ 9. Determines cause and effect.

____ 10. Summarizes information.

A NOTE ON THE IEP

If you have to write Individual Educational Plans, the list of reading skills and the three hundred activities in this book will be helpful. You can rewrite any of them in behavioral terms setting your own performance criteria.

Looking first at the list of skills by grade level (page 127-132), your first thought may be that there are more than fifteen word analysis skills taught in each primary grade. There can be hundreds depending on how they are listed, but you will find that the fifteen do cover all essential skills. When writing an IEP, it may be necessary to break these down into smaller units, or think of it as making a task analysis. What do students need to be able to do, for example, before they can "write independently the initial consonant of any word beginning with *b, c, d, f,* etc.," listed as the fourth word analysis skill at the first reader level? One thing they have to be able to do is hear those sounds. That skill is not listed, but it may be necessary for an IEP. The following are examples:

The major objective might be stated, "By the end of the second report period, the learner will write independently and correctly, the initial consonant of any word dictated by a teacher." Short term objectives can be written using the nine word analysis activities (60-68) that focus on initial consonant sounds.

Activity 60 — By the end of September, working less than half an hour, the learner will make an "Initial Sound Poster" independently for these consonants *b, d, f,* and *m* using at least three pictures for each sound.

Activity 61 — During the third week of September, the learner will make a collage of magazine pictures to illustrate the sound of *r* in the initial position.

Activity 62 — By the end of October, given the consonants *b, d, g,* and *p* and twenty pictures of objects whose names begin with those sounds, the learner will match pictures to letters within five minutes with 100% accuracy.

Activity 63 — By the end of October the learner will draw a picture which will contain at least five objects whose names begin with the sound of *t*.

Activity 64 — By the end of October, given a picture of a fish, the learner will write at least five words under the picture that begin like fish.

Activity 65 — By the second week of November, given twenty pictures of objects whose names begin with *j, l, m,* and *n,* labeled except for the first consonant, the learner will instantly write the correct initial consonant when given the pictures one at a time.

Activity 66 — By the second week of November, given a story that was dictated by the learner in early October in which all initial consonants have been deleted, the learner will correctly write in all the missing consonants in ten minutes.

Activity 67 — During the second report period, whenever the learner asks how to spell a word, the learner will supply the correct initial consonant 90% of the time.

Activity 68 — By the end of the second report period, the learner will write a sentence containing at least five words, each of which begin with any of the following fifteen consonants: *b, c, d, f, g, h, j, k, l, m, n, p, r, s, t.*

SOURCES OF INFORMATION ON LEARNING DISABILITIES

SOURCES OF INFORMATION ON LEARNING DISABILITIES

ORGANIZATIONS

ACLD (Association for Children and Adults with Learning Disabilities). 4156 Library Road, Pittsburgh, Pennsylvania 15234.

DCLD (Division for Children with Learning Disabilities of the Council of Exceptional Children). 1920 Association Drive, Reston, Virginia 22091

The Orton Society
8415 Bellona Lane, Towson, Maryland 21204

JOURNALS

Academic Therapy
20 Commercial Boulevard, Novato, California 94947

Journal of Learning Disabilities
101 East Ontario Street, Chicago, Illinois 60611

BOOKS WRITTEN BY AND/OR FOR PARENTS AND CHILDREN

Albert, Louise. *But I'm Ready to Go.* N.Y.: Dell, 1978.

Bierbauer, Elaine. *If Your Child Has a Learning Disability.* Danville, Illinois: Interstate Printers and Publishers, 1974.

Blue, Rose. *Me and Einstein: Breaking Through the Reading Barrier.* N.Y.: Human Science Press, 1979.

Brutten, Milton, Sylvia Richardson, and Charles Mangel. *Something's Wrong With My Child: A Parent's Book About Children With Learning Disabilities.* N.Y.: Harcourt, Brace, Jovanovich, 1973.

Clarke, Louise. *Can't Read, Can't Write, Can't Talk Too Good Either: How to Recognize and Overcome Dyslexia in Your Child.* Baltimore: Penguin Books, 1974.

Cohen, Martin. *Bets Wishz Doc.* N.Y.: Arthur Fields Books, 1974.

Crevor, J. W. Patrick. *Lost For Words.* Baltimore: Penguin Books.

Crosby, R.M.N. and R.A. Liston. *The Waysiders: A New Approach to Reading and the Dyslexic Child.* N.Y.: Delacorte Press, 1968.

Ellingson, C.C. *The Shadow Children: A Book About Children's Learning Disorders.* Chicago: Topaz Books, 1967.

Freeman, Stephen W. *Does Your Child Have a Disability? Questions Answered For Parents.* Springfield, Ilinois: Charles C. Thomas, 1974.

Gardner, Richard A. *MBD: The Family Book About Minimal Brain Dysfunction.* N.Y.: Jason Aronson, Inc., 1973.

Golden, Charles J. and Sandra Anderson. *Learning Disabilities and Brain Dysfunction: An Introduction For Educators and Parents.* Springfield, Illinois: Charles C. Thomas, 1979.

Hays, Marnell. *Oh Dear, Somebody Said 'Learning Disabilities!'* Novato, CA: Academic Therapy Publications, 1975.

Jones, Beverly and Jane Hart. *Where's Hannah.* N.Y.: Hart Publishing Co., 1968.

Levy, Harold B. *Square Pegs, Round Holes.* Boston: Little, Brown and Co., 1973.

Lewis, Richard, A. Strauss and Laura Lehtinen. *The Other Child: A Book For Parents and Laymen.* N.Y.: Grune and Stratton, 1960.

Miller, Julano. *Helping Your LD Child At Home.* Novato, CA: Academic Therapy Publications, 1973.

Osmon, Betty B. *Learning Disabilities: A Family Affair.* N.Y.: Random House, 1979.

Ostergren, Patricia G. *I'm Learning Disabled?* (Pamphlet) Janesville, Wisconsin: Center for Speech and Learning.

Smith, Sally. *No Easy Answers — The Learning Disabled Child.* Washington, D.C.: U.S. Gov't. Printing Office, 1979.

Wagner, Rudolph. *Dyslexia and Your Child: A Guide For Parents and Teachers.* N.Y.: Harper and Row, 1971.

Wender, Paul. *The Hyperactive Child: A Handbook For Parents.* N.Y.: Crown Publishers, 1973.

Williams, Beverly S. *Your Child Has a Learning Disability ... What Is It?* (Pamphlet) Chicago: The National Easter Seal Society for Crippled Children and Adults, 1971.

PROFESSIONAL BOOKS

Bannatyne, A. *Language, Reading, and Learning Disabilities: Psychology, Neuropsychology, Diagnosis, and Remediation.* Springfield, Ill.: Charles C. Thomas, 1971.

Benton, Arthur L. and David Pearl. *Dyslexia: An Appraisal of Current Knowledge.* N.Y.: Oxford Univ. Press, 1978.

Bryan, T. and J. Bryan. *Understanding Learning Disabilities.* Port Washington, N.Y.: Alfred Pub. Co., 1978.

Bush, Wilma Jo and Kenneth W. Waugh. *Diagnosing Learning Disabilities* (2nd Ed.). Columbus, Ohio: Charles E. Merrill, 1976.

Chaiken, William and Mary Joyce Harper. *Mainstreaming the Learning Disabled Adolescent: A Staff Development Guide.* Springfield, Ill.: Charles C. Thomas, 1979.

Critchley, MacDonald. *Developmental Dyslexia.* Springfield, Ill.: Charles C. Thomas, 1964.

Critchley, MacDonald. *The Dyslexic Child.* Springfield, Ill.: Charles C. Thomas, 1970.

Cruickshank, William M. *Approaches to Learning: The Best of ACLD* (Vol. 1), *Bridges to Tomorrow: The Best of ACLD* (Vol. 2). Syracuse, N.Y.: Syracuse Univ. Press, 1980.

Cruickshank, William. *The Brain-Injured Child in Home, School, and Community.* Syracuse, N.Y.: Syracuse Univ. Press, 1967.

deQuiros, Julio B. and O.L. Schrager. *Neuropsychological Fundamentals in Learning Disabilities.* (Rev.) Novato, CA: Academic Therapy Publications, 1980.

Farnham-Diggory, Sylvia. *Learning Disabilities: A Psychological Perspective.* Cambridge, Mass.: Harvard Univ. Press, 1978.

Frierson, F.C. and Walter Barbe. *Educating Children With Learning Disabilities: Selected Readings.* N.Y.: Appleton-Century Crofts, 1967.

Grzynkowicz, Wineva. *Basic Education For Children With Learning Disabilities.* Springfield, Ill.: Charles C. Thomas, 1979.

Hallahan, D. and William Cruickshank. *Psycho-Educational Foundations of Learning Disabilities.* Englewood Cliffs, N.J.: Prentice-Hall, 1973.

Hallahan D. and J. Kauffman. *Introduction to Learning Disabilities.* Englewood Cliffs, N.J.: Prentice-Hall, 1976.

Hammill, Donald and N. Bartel (Eds.). *Educational Perspectives in Learning Disabilities.* N.Y.: John Wiley & Sons, 1971.

Johnson, Doris and Helmer Myklebust. *Learning Disabilities: Educational Principles and Practices.* N.Y.: Grune and Stratton, 1967.

Johnson, S. and R. Morashy. *Learning Disabilities.* Boston: Allyn and Bacon, 1977.

Jordan, Dale R. *Dyslexia in the Classroom.* Columbus, Ohio: Charles E. Merrill, 1960.

Kephart, Newell C. *The Brain Injured Child in the Classroom.* Chicago: National Society for Crippled Children and Adults, 1963.

Kirk, Samuel A. *Educating Exceptional Children.* Boston: Houghton-Mifflin, 1972.

Klasen, Edith. *The Syndrome of Specific Dyslexia.* Baltimore: Univ. Park Press, 1972.

Kranes, Judith Ehre. *The Hidden Handicap.* N.Y.: Simon and Schuster, 1980.

Lerner, Janet. *Learning Disabilities: Theories, Diagnosis, and Teaching Strategies* (3rd Ed.). Boston: Houghton-Mifflin, 1980.

Mann, Lester, Libby Goodman and J. Lee Wiederholt. *Teaching the Learning-Disabled Adolescent.* Boston: Houghton-Mifflin, 1978.

McCarthy, James and Joan F. McCarthy. *Learning Disabilities.* Boston: Allyn and Bacon, 1969.

Mercer, L.D. *Children and Adolescents With Learning Disabilities.* Columbus, Ohio: Charles E. Merrill, 1979.

Money, John. (Ed.) *Reading Disability: Progress and Research Needs in Dyslexia.* Baltimore: The Johns Hopkins Press, 1962.

Money, John. *The Disabled Reader: Education of the Dyslexic Child.* Baltimore: The Johns Hopkins Press, 1966.

Myklebust, H.R. (Ed.) *Progress in Learning Disabilities.* (Four Volumes) N.Y.: Grune and Stratton, 1968, 1971, 1975, and 1978.

Ross, Alan O. *Learning Disability: The Unrealized Potential.* N.Y.: McGraw-Hill, 1977.

Valett, Robert E. *Dyslexia: A Neuropsychological Approach to Educating Children With Severe Reading Disorders.* Belmont, California: Fearon Pitman Publishers, 1980.

Valett, Robert. *The Remediation of Learning Disabilities.* Belmont, California: Fearon Pitman Publishers, 1974.

Wallace, G. and J.A. McLoughlin. *Learning Disabilities: Concepts and Characteristics* (2nd ed.). Columbus, Ohio: Charles E. Merrill, 1979.

Wiig, Elisabeth H. and J.M. Kaufman. *Introduction to Learning Disabilities: A Psycho-Behavioral Approach.* Englewood Cliffs, N.J.: Prentice-Hall, 1976.

Wiig, Elisabeth H. and Eleanor M. Semel. *Language Disabilities in Children and Adolescents.* Columbus, Ohio: Charles E. Merrill, 1976.

ABOUT THE AUTHOR

Dorothy Raymond is Director of Reading and a school psychologist in the Waterville, Maine, public school system. She has spent more than twenty years helping teachers and tutors make reading enjoyable by using creative and individualized approaches. She has given workshops and in-service training and has taught university courses from elementary reading to clinical practices in learning disabilities.